White Privilege

Introducing Polity's new series:
little books that make you THINK.

Quassim Cassam, *Conspiracy Theories*
Stephen Mumford, *Football*
Shannon Sullivan, *White Privilege*

Shannon Sullivan

White Privilege

polity

The right of Shannon Sullivan to be identified as Author of this Work has been asserted in accordance with the UK Copyright, Designs and Patents Act 1988.

First published in 2019 by Polity Press

Reprinted 2020

Polity Press
65 Bridge Street
Cambridge CB2 1UR, UK

Polity Press
101 Station Landing
Suite 300
Medford, MA 02155, USA

ISBN-13: 978-1-5095-3528-6
ISBN-13: 978-1-5095-3529-3(pb)

A catalogue record for this book is available from the British Library.

Typeset in 11 on 15 Sabon by
Servis Filmsetting Ltd, Stockport, Cheshire
Printed and bound in the United States by LSC Communications

The publisher has used its best endeavors to ensure that the URLs for external websites referred to in this book are correct and active at the time of going to press. However, the publisher has no responsibility for the websites and can make no guarantee that a site will remain live or that the content is or will remain appropriate.

Every effort has been made to trace all copyright holders, but if any have been overlooked the publisher will be pleased to include any necessary credits in any subsequent reprint or edition.

For further information on Polity, visit our website:

Library of Congress Cataloging - in - Publication Data

Names: Sullivan, Shannon, 1967- author.

Title: White privilege / Shannon Sullivan.

Description: Cambridge, UK ; Medford, MA : Polity, 2019. | Includes
bibliographical references. | Summary: "Some embrace the idea of white privilege as an important concept that helps us to make sense of the connection between race and social and political disadvantages, while others are critical or even hostile. Philosopher Shannon Sullivan cuts through the confusion and cross - talk to challenge what 'everybody knows' about white privilege". -- Provided by publisher.

Identifiers: LCCN 2019009945 (print) | LCCN 2019980333 (ebook) | ISBN
9781509535286 (hardback) | ISBN 9781509535293 (paperback) | ISBN
9781509535309 (epub)

Subjects: LCSH: Whites -- Race identity -- United States. | Whites -- United
States -- Psychology. | Privilege (Social psychology) -- United States. |
United States -- Race relations.

Classification: LCC E184.A1 S9543 2019 (print) | LCC E184.A1 (ebook) |
DDC 305.809 -- dc23

LC record available at https://lccn.loc.gov/2019009945

LC ebook record available at https://lccn.loc.gov/2019980333

Contents

Introduction

What "everybody knows" about white privilege

The idea of white privilege seems to be everywhere nowadays. At least since 2014, with the police shooting of unarmed Black teenager Michael Brown in Ferguson, Missouri, and the subsequent birth of the Black Lives Matter movement, it is no longer a topic confined to academic study.[1] From *Harry Potter* star Emma Watson's 2018 confession of her white privilege to Black Lives Matter's criticism of white Philadelphians who damaged property after their team's 2018 Super Bowl victory, white people's racial privilege is being talked about by white and non-white people alike. It even has its own

---

[1] I will capitalize "Black" when discussing people of the African diaspora and use "black" simply to indicate a color. I will use lower case "white" for white people since they have not (yet) really figured out a racial identity apart from white supremacy and white privilege, and for that reason, capitalizing "White" would be misleading and/ or confusing for my purposes here.

Introduction

Twitter hashtag (#whiteprivilege). Not all of the talk about white privilege has the goal of eliminating it, however. Some of it questions whether white privilege exists and accuses people of color of making up the idea to get an unfair advantage over white people. Some of it accuses white people instead, charging elite whites with using the idea of white privilege to assert their moral superiority by shaming poor and working-class white people. In all the talk and crosstalk about white privilege, it's not always clear whether people even mean the same thing when they criticize, support, and/or reject the term. So, what exactly *is* white privilege and how should we make sense of the various and often conflicting things said about it? And if it does exist, what should—or can—be done about it?

The goal of this book is to clarify what white privilege is and what it is not. It aims to unsettle pat assumptions about white privilege, and these are assumptions held both by those who are "for" and by those who are "against" white privilege. I do not want to preach to the choir of those who oppose white privilege; down that road lies the problem of white people's smug self-congratulation. But neither will I throw out the concept of white privilege because of the confusions that surround it. Down that road lies the problem of white people's dismissal of race and racism as trivial, even nonexistent. I think that white privilege exists and that in addition to harming people of color, it dehumanizes white people. (More on the latter claim in Chapter 5.) But I also think that there are important things to learn from people who are skeptical about the notion. Above all, I am aware that stating my opposition to white privilege could seem like white virtue signaling, as if my goal is to assure readers that I'm one of the "good white people," when I think good white people are a big part of the problem. Ultimately, I would like to persuade skeptics of white privilege *and* to shake up many treasured ideas held by so-called true believers. And so, I find myself asking, how can we cut through the fog of white defensiveness and white self-righteousness to get to a useful understanding of what white privilege is?

To answer this question, I examine beliefs about white privilege that might seem obviously true, but which I will argue are false in some important way. For example, is white privilege only about race? I will argue, somewhat counterintuitively, that a big part of the answer is no. Likewise, is the point of recognizing white privilege to get rid of it? I also will argue that, in a significant sense, the answer is no. In that way, this book aims for a kind of Socratic wisdom/ignorance concerning white privilege. The ancient Greek philosopher Socrates claimed that genuine wisdom is not found in knowing a large number of things. It instead is found in knowing what you don't know. Realizing that we don't actually know many of the things that we believe to be true about white privilege is what can lead to a greater understanding of it. Doing so, however, means taking seriously ideas or beliefs that can seem unwise or unpopular to hold, and that can be risky. (In fact, Socrates was sentenced to death for questioning the "wise" people and ideas that reigned in Athens in his day.) I ask you to take some existential risks with me in reading this book. While they won't be as dangerous as the ones that Socrates faced, I should caution you that this is not a feel-good book.

While many of the examples in this book will draw from the United States, white privilege is not merely "an American thing." That assumption also is one of the things that "everybody knows" across the globe: The United States is where racism, white supremacy, and white privilege run rampant. Race, and whiteness in particular, supposedly are not very relevant in Canada and western European countries, for example, some of which (like France) recently have removed all reference to race in their constitution. They did this since race is a social construction and therefore supposedly isn't real. The belief that race and white privilege are exclusively American things dumps problems of racism onto the United States. Treating the U.S. as "that racial hellhole on the other side of the Atlantic" is an easy way for European countries to avoid looking at their own distinctive forms of racism and white privilege (Fleming 2018, 83). And European countries do have them, as examples in this book will show. The more that we "know" the United States is uniquely home to persistent problems of white privilege, the more we don't understand white privilege.

Each of the book's five chapters is titled with a supposed truth about white privilege. They build from definitions of white privilege, including the complicated issue of who has it (Chapters 1–2), to questions about action, including what can or should be done about white privilege (Chapters 3–5). While I hope that white readers will find this book particularly relevant to their lives, its analyses of white privilege should be informative and useful for readers of all races. For all readers, but perhaps for white readers in particular, I also want to underscore that the goal of this book is not to make white people feel guilty. While Chapter 3 will discuss white guilt in more detail, let me say here that I think that white guilt tends to be a red herring. Like the fish whose strong smell can throw trained dogs off the scent they are tracking, white guilt often distracts white people from the important question of what they can do to counter white privilege.

Having said that, however, it's also important to emphasize that not feeling guilty is *not* the same thing as feeling confident and assured. This book is likely to make all readers, and perhaps especially white readers, uncomfortable. Questioning settled "truths" about white privilege can leave people unsure what to believe and what to do with regard to ongoing issues of race and racism. This is just as true for people of color as it is for white people. People of color might become less certain rather than more certain, for example, concerning how white people could be helpful partners in struggles for racial justice. This might sound like something to avoid: whatever their race, who wants to feel uneasy and unsure about fundamentally important questions? But unsettling feelings should not be avoided just because they are unsettling. If what we "know" to be true about white privilege often is wrong or incomplete in some significant respects, then feeling a bit disoriented and lost is a good first step toward finding a different way to address the issue.[2]

[2] I wish to thank my editor at Polity, Pascal Porcheron, copyeditor Ann Klefstad, and two anonymous reviewers for helpful feedback on earlier versions of this book.

1

"White privilege is only about race"

Nothing could seem more obvious than the belief that white privilege is about race. Isn't white privilege about white people having unfair advantages because of their whiteness? Take the example of white people's ability to browse in a department store without being tailed by undercover security guards. Black people in the United States often report being surreptitiously followed in public spaces such as this, treated as implicitly criminal, while white people generally do not have that experience. Isn't this an example of social advantage that white people have over Black people because of their different races?

The answer is "yes" in that white people's race is an important factor in white privilege. But it also is "no" in that white privilege is just as much about the middle-to-upper-class privilege of certain white people as it is about their race. We misunderstand white privilege if we try to separate race and class to focus only on race. Many examples of white privilege are better understood as white *class* privilege. We should not assume that poor and working-class white people benefit from white privilege in the same ways that middle-to-upper-class white people do.

That does not mean, however, that poor and working-class white people never benefit from their whiteness. We misunderstand white privilege in the opposite way if we reduce race to class and think that white privilege is really only about economic and educational privilege. When it comes to white privilege, race and class are inevitably entangled. They cannot be reduced to each other, and this holds true not just for white people but also for people of color. (More on people of color and white privilege in the next chapter.) This chapter focuses on the tangle of race and class in white people's lives and demonstrates how white privilege is not just about whiteness.

* * *

White privilege tends to be found in places and spaces where laws don't apply. Benefitting from white privilege generally is not illegal, in other words, and that's one of the things that gives it so much power. It operates outside explicit legal codification. This makes white privilege different from the racial advantages that white people had when discrimination against Black people and other people of color was legal, as it was in the United States, South Africa, and other countries well into the latter half of the twentieth century. There were laws explicitly naming race that could be fought or defended or whatever—but in any case, it was clear that they existed. They could be identified, pointed to, reckoned with.

That all changed with the end of Jim Crow, apartheid, and other laws legalizing racial discrimination and segregation. When it became illegal to grant social, educational, financial, and other advantages to white people, white people's racial advantages became more difficult to identify. Many white people thought that perhaps those advantages really had been eliminated and the new laws were working to ensure equal opportunity no matter what one's race. (Note that I did not say "equality," as if the new laws assumed that all individuals and their aptitudes were the same. This sometimes is how anti-discrimination laws are criticized, even ridiculed, for allegedly operating with a fundamental misunderstanding of human nature.) For example, it could easily seem that equal opportunity for all races was achieved in the United States in the 1950s and 1960s if you are looking for racial advantages and disadvantages in their old forms. Black people don't have to ride at the back of the bus or use "colored" water fountains anymore. But looking for racial advantage in that form today as evidence of white privilege is like looking for horse-drawn carriages on the highway as evidence of transportation. There isn't anything there. Or so it might seem—because what you are looking for is a barrier to seeing what *is* there. Just as there are all kinds of horsepower on roads today that don't look like the horsepower of yesteryear, there are all kinds of implicit white privileges that don't look like the legalized white advantages and open white supremacy of yesterday. Of course, there still are examples of open white supremacy to be found today, just as there still are horse-drawn carriages on some roads. That does not change the fact that for the most part, white racial advantage has radically—and deceptively—changed its form. This is how it has survived, how it has ensured its ongoing existence amid a great deal of social change.

What do those implicit, extralegal racial privileges look like? Consider two real-life examples that recently happened to me or to people I know:

"White privilege is only about race"

(1) I was pulled over in my hometown for speeding one recent Sunday afternoon, driving an older hybrid SUV and dressed in jeans, looking like a harried suburban mom rushing to the grocery store between the kids' events (which I was). While I didn't realize the extent to which I was speeding—57 mph on a road that had dropped from 55 mph to 35 mph some distance back from where I was—I instantly knew what the problem was when I saw the officer's flashing lights behind me. After examining my license and asking me if I had a good driving record as I murmured an apology about rushing to the grocery store, the white male officer let me go with a warning and no ticket or court appearance. (I was so far over the speed limit that a court appearance would have been mandatory if he had ticketed me.)

(2) A colleague of mine who is African American, "Melinda" (a pseudonym), recently flew on a major airline in the United States that now requires passengers to pay extra for luggage space in the overhead bin. She was dressed professionally, ready for the academic event that she was attending. Her husband, who is white, had flown on the same airline the week before and told her not to worry about it. The carry-on bag he used was the same one she would use, and they let him carry it on without quibbling

11

over whether it was an inch too long. When Melinda tried to board the plane, however, the gate agents very precisely applied the sizing rules to her bag and would not let her carry it on. She had to pay $50 at the gate to check the bag instead.

In each of these situations, nothing illegal happened. And in each of them, white people benefitted from their whiteness, giving them an advantage over people of color. Police officers and airline gate attendants are allowed to use discretion in their jobs, deciding, for example, when to strictly apply the laws or rules and when to bend them or let someone go with a warning. That is not necessarily a bad thing. It's hard to imagine a world in which every situation encountered in a job could or should be governed by an explicit rule. Frankly, that kind of world sounds like bureaucratic hell. Using discretion isn't the problem. The problem is using it unfairly to benefit one racial group over others.

This often isn't a conscious decision. I doubt that the police officer who stopped me consciously thought to himself, "Hmm, she's white, so I think I'll cut her some slack." I also doubt that the gate attendant consciously said to herself, "I'm going to let the white people on the plane with their slightly oversized bags, but not the Black ones."

"White privilege is only about race"

Decisions to privilege white people instead tend to be made unconsciously, without explicitly invoking race. They often are made by "good" people who wouldn't consider themselves to be racist or to be privileging white people at all (Sullivan 2006 and 2014). In my case, the officer likely saw me as a relatively harmless person who was just having a stressful day, not a dangerous lawbreaker. And in Melinda's case, the gate attendant likely saw her—but not her white husband—as an aggressive rule breaker, someone who was trying to get away with something that wasn't allowed.

That difference gets at the heart of white privilege: white people generally are seen as embodying a society's standards of truth and goodness. (And standards of beauty, it should be added, although I will not discuss the aesthetics of white privilege much here. For more on this topic, see Robinson 2011.) White people generally are perceived as upstanding, law-abiding citizens while people of color—particularly Black and Hispanic/Latinx people, at least in the United States—tend to be seen as criminals. This perception is independent of the particular situation; in fact, it often shapes how a particular situation is understood. If a white person breaks the law or rule, it is a sign that a law-abiding person needs a little reminder of what the law or rule is. But if a Black person breaks the law or rule, it confirms their inherent criminality, which existed before the law or rule was broken and which the broken law or rule merely revealed. White privilege means being given the benefit of the doubt because a white person is (seen as) trustworthy and respectable.

Of course, in an ideal world, all people would receive respect and be treated as trustworthy unless they did something to violate that respect and trust. My point is not that there is something inherently wrong with respecting or trusting white people. We might say that being treated respectfully ought to be a basic, unearned entitlement that every person has a right to (McIntosh 1989). What is wrong is when trust and respect are granted to some people and denied to others because of their race (or other social categories, for that matter). In that case, an unearned entitlement has been made into an unearned advantage, and the rights of people of color to the entitlement have been violated (Zack 2015).

I admit that it's impossible for me to prove that white privilege is why I didn't receive a ticket or why Melinda's husband was allowed to board the plane with an oversized bag and she was not. I cannot demonstrate "beyond a reasonable doubt," as the U.S. legal system says, that other factors weren't more important. Maybe the officer was just in a good mood that particular Sunday. Maybe on the day that Melinda was traveling the flight attendant had been reprimanded by her boss for letting too many carry-on bags on the plane. Almost every claim about the existence of white privilege is open to the criticism that a person is just imagining or exaggerating things. Or worse, the criticism sometimes is that a person is "playing the race card," that is, injecting race into a situation where it doesn't exist. To try to identify white privilege in a situation can make you feel a bit paranoid. (It also can make you the target of anything from mild to severe gaslighting.) This isn't too surprising, however, given that white privilege operates outside of official regulations and statutes. It is "invisible" in that sense. Trying to show or convince others that it exists can sometimes make you feel like you're questioning reality—which in fact you are doing, but that doesn't make you crazy.

Let me raise a different doubt about what happened in my and Melinda's situations, however. Would a poor white person driving a rundown car have been let off the hook for speeding? Would they have been allowed to board a plane with a bag that was slightly oversized? There's a good chance that the answer to these questions is "no." Not all white people are given the same benefit of the doubt. So-called white trash often are not treated or respected as upstanding citizens in the same way that middle-to-upper-class white people are. They often are criminalized before the fact, and they generally are not seen as the moral, aesthetic, or other standardbearers of society. In the late 1960s, for example, self-identified white hillbillies in Chicago formed the Young Patriots Organization to fight police brutality within poor white neighborhoods, joining forces at one point in this fight with the Black Panther Party and the Puerto Rican Young Lords in what they termed a Rainbow Coalition (Sonnie and Tracy 2011). Flash forward to 2018, and white men in their twenties riding around in pickup trucks in rural North Carolina likewise are hassled by the police all the time, as one of my white male students recently pointed out. On the aesthetic side, poor rural white people often are ridiculed for the way they look, talk, and dress. Consider the "crazy hillbilly teeth" that you can buy for your Halloween costume, giving you "the jacked dentures of a hick . . . to finish your hilarious look," complete with tattered overalls and a jug of moonshine (Spirit n.d.). Poor white people generally don't count as standardbearers of society.

"White privilege is only about race"

That privilege is reserved for middle-to-upper-class white people. For that reason, white privilege is best thought of as white *class* privilege. It is a privilege that comes with education, money, and the lifestyle and personal appearance that both of those provide.

In that case, is white class privilege really *white* class privilege? Maybe it is simply class privilege that has been mistaken for racial privilege. The initial version of Peggy McIntosh's seminal essay on "White Privilege: Unpacking the Invisible White Knapsack" has been criticized along these lines. When she listed everyday instances of white privilege in her life, "unearned assets that [she] could count on cashing in each day" as she called them, many of those instances struck her readers as examples of class privilege instead (McIntosh 1989, 10). For example, claims that "If I should need to move, I can be pretty sure of renting or purchasing housing in an area which I can afford and in which I want to live" and "I can be pretty sure of finding a publisher for this piece on white privilege" speak just as much, if not more, about financial and educational privileges than they do about racial privileges (1989, 10–11). Class privilege shows up as a feature of most if not all racial groups in which members with "more"—more money, education, or whatever else is valued in society—are treated better than those with "less." For that reason, we might think that white class privilege actually is an *intra*group pattern of advantage and disadvantage among whites, rather than an *inter*group pattern that gives white people a leg up over non-white people. After all, many Black middle-class and upper-middle-class people also go to great lengths to make sure that they are not mistaken for the Black poor in public spaces: when they are shopping, working, walking or driving in town, and so on (Lacy 2007). A similar pattern can be found with middle-to-upper-class Hispanic/Latinx people in the United States, who can "protect" themselves from being seen as illegal immigrants by ensuring that they are not identified as poor (Masuoka and Junn 2013).

But these are not equivalent situations. For starters, wealth and education—even fame—do not necessarily protect Black people from racial discrimination and assault, as the examples of James Blake and Henry Louis Gates, Jr., show. Blake is a now-retired international tennis star who was tackled and handcuffed by police on the streets of New York in 2015 when an officer was looking for a Black man who had committed a crime in the area. In addition to mistaking Blake for the suspect merely because Blake is Black, the officer was found to have used excessive force when he arrested him (Goodman

2015). Gates is a distinguished Harvard University professor and public intellectual who was arrested on the porch of his own Boston-area home in 2009 when trying to force open the door he was locked out of after a neighbor reported someone trying to break into the house. The neighbor's reaction might be understandable—yet why didn't she recognize her own neighbor, we might wonder?—but the police officer's response is not. Even after asking for and seeing Gates' identification, the officer arrested Gates for disorderly conduct—which means disrupting or inconveniencing *the public*—because Gates was yelling at the officer to leave while they were *inside* Gates's private home. Contrast Gates's experience with that of a white journalist who also lived near Harvard and recently was helping a white neighbor who had locked herself out of her house. When a Cambridge police officer happened by, he helped steady the ladder that they were using to access a second-story porch. He never once asked the white women for proof that one of them lived in the house (Coates 2010). These examples illustrate how class privilege does not necessarily protect Black people from being criminalized because of their race or give them the privilege of being assumed to be an innocent bystander or a person in need of help. The class privilege that some white people have does not seamlessly transfer to middle-to-upper-class people of color.

On top of that, white people without high socio-economic status can and do still benefit from their whiteness. The way they benefit from whiteness often looks different than it does for middle-to-upper-class white people, but their racial privilege still exists. For example, even if some people of color have more (of whatever is being measured or valued) than some white people, this "truth" misleadingly compares people of color and white people at different class levels. In contrast, if we compare groups of people at the same class level in the United States, we see that at every level of class, white people do better than Hispanic/Latinx people and especially African American and Indigenous people (Gathright 2018). This pattern is evident not just in economic matters (such as salaries and savings), but also in education (such as long-term suspension rates) and in health outcomes (such as preterm birth and infant mortality rates) (Hayes-Greene and Love 2016). In those ways, even the poorest white people have some white privilege.

I admit that the word "privilege" can sound off-target and perhaps off-putting in this context. As one poor white person reacted when she first heard someone say that she was racially privileged,

"White privilege is only about race"

"THE F&CK!?!? . . . my white skin didn't do shit to prevent me from experiencing poverty" (Crosley-Corcoran 2014). The everyday sense of the word "privilege" can make it sound like it's about the upper crust of society. The word comes off like a description of a select group of people who were born with silver spoons in their mouths. This is why some scholars have struggled to find a different word to describe what poor white people's racial advantages are (see, for example, Sullivan 2017). Whatever word we use, however, we need a way to recognize that poor and so-called lower-class white people benefit from their race at times.

One way they benefit is through their citizenship. As poor as Crosley-Corcoran was growing up in the United States, living in a camper without heat or running water, she never faced deportation. She also never faced the possibility of having her parents deported and leaving her without caregivers or in foster care. Unlike many poor Hispanic/Latinx families, she was not terrorized by ICE (Immigration and Customs Enforcement) raids that targeted Latinx and Hispanic neighborhoods in an effort to identify and capture suspected "illegals." Indeed, no matter how poor a white person is, no matter how much they are identified as "white trash," they have the privilege of being assumed to belong in the United

States. This is a sharply different situation from that of Latinx and Hispanics. Because illegal immigration generally is perceived in the United States as Hispanic/Latinx—perhaps especially Mexican, depending on what part of the country you are in—Latinx and Hispanics, no matter their citizenship status, often are stereotyped as "illegals" (Masuoka and Junn 2013). A vicious equation rules in which immigrant = illegal immigrant = Hispanic/Latinx. (Increasingly in the United States and Western Europe, this equation also applies to anyone who looks "Muslim," even though Islam is a religion, not a race.) In these ways, Hispanics and Latinx are identified as "lawbreakers," justifying ICE and other police procedures to punish them.

Deborah Foster, a white writer and educator, provides an additional example of the white privileges that poor white people sometimes have (Foster 2017). After being placed in foster care because her home didn't have sufficient heat or food, she was returned to her mother. Without even discussing the second chances Foster received from the school system after skipping too many classes, let me say that again: *the state returned her to her mother.* That fact might seem trivial, but in light of the workings of the child welfare system in the United States, it is not. It is a powerful example of white privilege. Even though she was dirt poor, Foster's mother, who was white, was assumed to be a competent-enough parent who should be allowed to resume care of her child once certain basic conditions were met. The state's intervention was less of an intrusion that broke up Foster's family than it was a helping hand to enable the family to get back on their feet again.

I recognize the trauma of having a child removed from the home even temporarily. In fact, even though Foster and her mother had some white privilege, their case helps us see an important way in which the white privilege of poor whites is less robust than that of middle-to-upper-class ones. The latter generally do not have the child welfare system involved in their lives, and this is not only because they have enough money to provide heat and food. It also is because middle-to-upper-class white people are given the benefit of the doubt if something dangerous or questionable happens to their child. Contrast Foster's experience with that of a middle-class white family in my small hometown in North Carolina. Early one weekday evening, all parents of the middle school received a text from the school principal concerning "Gina" (a pseudonym). Gina was a white sixth grader—who was not racially identified in the text, of course—who had gone home with a friend after school and whose mother was anxiously looking for her. We were instructed to reply to the principal if Gina had come to our house. A few minutes later we received a follow-up text thanking us for our prompt responses and letting us know that Gina had been located and was safely on her way home. Child protective services was not called to make sure that Gina's parents were responsible enough to maintain custody of their child. It was a mix-up that could have happened to anyone ... except that "anyone" turns out *not* to be everyone. It is those people of a particular race and class who are given the benefit of the doubt.

Now contrast both Foster's and Gina's parents' experience with that of many Black families, especially ones that are poor. Black children are being removed legally from their homes by the child welfare system at increasingly high rates—disproportionately much higher than the rates for white children. When they are, it is extremely difficult for their parents to get them back. Their parental rights often are terminated so that the "burden" of the children on the foster care system can be alleviated through the children's adoption. In addition to disrupting Black families, this process serves to feed the school-to-prison pipeline. Children in foster care are more likely than those who remain in their homes to leave school and become involved in the juvenile detention system, setting them up to enter the prison system as adults (Roberts 2002). The fact that Foster eventually was able to go back home was a precious privilege provided by her and her mother's whiteness, just as was the fact that Gina got to go home directly without any involvement by the child welfare system.

In sum, white privilege is never just about whiteness, even as we cannot leave whiteness out of the equation. Along with gender, citizenship, and other meaningful characteristics of contemporary human life, race and class are intersectional (Crenshaw 1991; May 2015). Each substantially impacts and helps constitute the other, which means that we can't adequately capture the complexity of race if we describe it in isolation from class, and vice versa. To underscore that point, let me conclude with another example of how race and class are entangled in white privilege:

(3) Two acquaintances of mine who are white, "Bill" and "Marie" (pseudonyms), sometimes have struggled to remain middle class. During one of those times of struggle, they couldn't make their mortgage payments and so they lost their house in the wake of the 2007–2008 recession in the United States. A white businessman

who owned real estate in their town was a fellow member of their church, and he offered to rent one of his rental houses to them so that they had a place to go after they were forced out of their house. They had to wait a week, however, until a current rental application for the house had expired. The Black woman who had applied to rent the house had one more week to provide a $500 security deposit, after which the landlord was no longer legally obligated to hold the house for her. After she missed the deadline, Bill and Marie immediately rented and moved into the house, and they were allowed to do so without providing a security deposit since they did not have enough cash on hand to cover it. (The Black woman contacted the landlord a week after the deadline to provide the $500 security deposit but found out that the house had already been rented.) Bill also needed a job to help make the rent, and the landlord was able to offer him an hourly wage position at a small business that he owned in town.

The first thing to note in this example is that a law was broken. While it is legal to refuse to rent to someone who cannot meet the legal terms of a lease, such as providing a security deposit, it violates Federal Fair Housing laws in the United States to apply different lease conditions based on different applicants' race. If the Black woman ever found out that Bill and Marie were allowed to rent the house without providing a security deposit, she could sue the landlord and I suspect that she would win. So, where is the white privilege in this example?

To begin, it is located in the landlord's unconscious—or perhaps even conscious—bias toward white people. In much the same way that I was viewed by the police officer as a responsible, trustworthy citizen, Bill and Marie were viewed by the landlord as reliable, trustworthy tenants. Even though they objectively were bigger financial risks than the Black woman was, they were given the lease. I admittedly haven't seen the full credit and criminal background reports on Bill and Marie, much less on the Black woman (whom I don't know). But I do know this: she could come up with the $500 cash deposit, even if it took a few extra days, while Bill and Marie could not. In addition, Bill did not have a paying job at the time of their rental application. On paper, so to speak, Bill and Marie were the weaker applicants and should have been turned down. Their whiteness got them a place to live. They might not have had much class privilege, but their whiteness still helped them land on their feet.

A second, related place that we can see white privilege in this example brings out its complex relationships with class. Bill and Marie didn't *directly* have white class privilege; that better describes the wealthy businessman and landlord. Bill and Marie were struggling, they were suffering, and their whiteness didn't prevent them from losing their house. But they had connections with financially stable, even wealthy white people in town, and they were able to benefit from those people's class privilege. Other people's white class privilege and better financial position provided Bill and Marie with a social safety net in the form of other white people with resources, even if they might not have known about it prior to being evicted from their home. This doesn't mean that all white people automatically land on their feet because of their white privilege, but it does mean that they have a much greater chance of doing so, even if they are struggling or poor.

We can view Bill and Marie's whiteness as what psychologists call an implicit affordance (Gibson 1979). An affordance is what a particular environment provides an animal, including human animals. The more affordances, the better the fit between environment and animal, and thus the more likely it is that the animal will thrive. Bill and Marie's whiteness was a way that they matched their social environment, making it a good fit for them and helping them survive. While wealthy white people generally have more affordances than poor white people do, in a society that prizes whiteness all white people have some racial affordances, at least some of the time. In the form of their church membership, the business arrangements in the town, and other aspects of their hometown, Bill and Marie lived in a world that generally was suited to them, even as they struggled financially. They had relationships with people in the community who had the means and the will to provide Bill and Marie a second chance. They are working-class white people who were given the benefit of the doubt. Like their landlord, they are white people with white privilege.

2

"Only white people have white privilege"

One reason that white privilege is so complex is that white people are not all the same. Class differences among white people make a big difference in how and when white people benefit from their whiteness. Gender also makes a big difference. White men and white women often are granted very different advantages and affordances due to their race. White middle-to-upper-class women tend to be seen as innocent and pure, for example, while white middle-to-upper-class men often are assumed to be intelligent and good leaders. But even if there are classed, gendered, and other variations in what white privilege looks like, it seems safe to say that only white people have it. Wouldn't it be logically contradictory, even oxymoronic—with a tongue-in-cheek emphasis on "moronic"—to claim that a Black person can have white privilege? By definition, doesn't white privilege exclude people who are not white?

In addition to logical problems, there would seem to be ethical problems with the claim that Black and other people of color can have white privilege. If people who are not white can benefit from white privilege, then haven't we drained the concept of white privilege of all meaning? Doesn't that flatten it out, making the concept useless? If in principle everyone can have white privilege, then does anyone—even a white person—*really* have it? After all, privilege (of any sort) is a thing that some people have and others do not. The claim that Black and other people of color can have white privilege could seem like a wily trick for white people to get themselves off the racial hook, leaving their white privilege intact even as they deny that they have it.

It's not a trick, however. Another reason that white privilege is so complex is that it is not limited to white people. We misunderstand white privilege if we think that Black and other people of color never have it. This chapter will examine how white privilege can cross racial lines *and* continue to benefit white people even as it does so. That last point is important, and I'll return to it at the end of the chapter. I also will analyze claims that Black, rather

31

than white, privilege is the real form of racial privilege that exists in the United States today.

*　*　*

Anna Holmes is an American writer with one Black and one white parent. Born in 1973, she is part of a generation of biracial children—"the Loving Generation"—who were born after the 1967 Supreme Court case *Loving v. Virginia*. That case invalidated state laws that prohibited interracial marriage, and the number of Black-white couples in the United States doubled within a decade or so as a result. As Holmes notes, many of the most successful and widely recognized Black people in the United States in the 2010s are part of the Loving Generation: actress Halle Berry, singer Mariah Carey, athlete Derek Jeter, and the Duchess of Sussex Meghan Markle, just to name a few. Even former U.S. President Barack Obama can be considered part of the leading edge of the Loving Generation. Although he was born six years before the *Loving* case, his father was Black and his mother was white, and he was reared by his mother and her white family. Like Holmes, Obama is connected to a civil rights era that produced "an entire generation of kids whose very existence symbolized racial progress for some, cultural impurity for others"

"Only white people have white privilege"

(Holmes 2018). This was a generation of non-white children whose close family members included white people.

As Holmes explains, her direct connection with whiteness has given her some white privilege. This is not because she attempts to "pass" as white. Holmes is light-skinned, but she identifies as Black. Her white privilege is found not in being or identifying as white, but instead in her implicit knowledge of white norms, sensibilities, and ways of doing things that came from living with and being accepted by white family members. To understand this particular kind of knowledge of whiteness—call it family familiarity—we need to distinguish it from at least two other kinds of relationships with whiteness. Let's begin with what I'll call survival knowledge. Black people have long had to understand how whiteness and white people operate in order to survive. If a Black domestic worker did not understand how to avoid insulting a white employer's ego, for example, she was likely to be punished severely and/or fired. In fact, Black people might understand white people better than white people understand themselves. In large part, this is because white people tend to refuse (often unconsciously) to reckon with the large role that race plays in their lives. As W. E. B. Du Bois famously argued, Black people are gifted/cursed with a double consciousness, an ability to see and understand the world from the perspective of both white Americans and African Americans. It is a curse because it is the product of racial oppression, but it simultaneously is a gift because of the understanding that it provides (Du Bois 1994). Survival knowledge of whiteness has been and continues to be very important to the lives of Black people and other people of color, but it is not the same thing as family familiarity. Survival knowledge lacks the genuinely loving relationship with a close white family member which family familiarity includes. I'll say more about this shortly.

The second kind of relationship with whiteness that we need to distinguish from family familiarity could be called ancestral ties to whiteness. Virtually all African American people in the United States have some distant white ancestry. Based on genetic testing done by five prominent DNA companies, for example, the average African American is genetically about 20–25 percent white European (Gates 2013). Individual variation can be quite a bit larger than this, ranging from as low as 3 percent to as high as 46 percent of white European "blood" in an African American. (The historical "one-drop" rule meant, of course, that no matter how high their percentage of white European "blood," a person with any sub-Saharan African "blood" still counted as Black.) The point is that virtually 100 percent of African Americans have ancestral ties to whiteness. This overwhelmingly is not because of Black-white couples who voluntarily partnered together. To be blunt, it is because of rape and other forms of sexual coercion. This took place mostly between Black women (slaves) and white men (masters). But it also sometimes occurred between white women and Black men, the latter of whom could be forced to engage in sex under the cruelly ironic threat that if he didn't do what the white woman wanted, she would accuse him of assaulting her. This was the type of terrorizing accusation that produced many of the lynchings of Black men in the nineteenth and twentieth centuries. Even though ancestral ties speak of sexual relationships between Black and white people, they are radically different from family familiarity. They occurred too far back in history and are too deeply embedded in situations of rape and sexual assault to be about a Black or biracial child's growing up in an immediate family that includes white people who love them.

The kind of white privilege generated by family familiarity with whiteness comes not from mere proximity to or a genetic tie with white people, but from a direct relationship with them in which a Black person is accepted and affirmed. That affirmation made it comfortable and natural for Holmes to interact with white people as she was growing up. Barack Obama also talks about his positive interactions with his white family members in a similar way (Fleming 2018, 99–100). Like Holmes, Obama moved among white family members with ease, and his sense of possibility in life was encouraged by white people who embraced and loved him. As Holmes describes it, her white privilege is found primarily in the ways of being, thinking, and interacting that formed her early on as a person, gained as a child living in a white world that nurtured them. This is a world that is not always or even often available to people of color.

In a complementary fashion, Holmes also benefits from white privilege because family familiarity with whiteness can make it easier for white people to identify with her. By that, I do not mean that white people necessarily know that Holmes has a white parent or that they consciously think about her race or family upbringing at all. Instead, I mean that Holmes's sense of ease and naturalness around white people and their white ways can make it easier for white people to feel comfortable around her. They can feel that "even though" she is a Black person, she is "just like us." Being perceived as similar to white people often leads to white people feeling more relaxed around people of color. That type of situation privileges Holmes by opening doors of opportunity for her, doors that are metaphorically (and sometimes literally) monitored by middle-to-upper-class white people or their affiliates. White people generally are more likely to open those doors for people with whom they feel comfortable. That probably is true for everyone, but it becomes problematic when one particular group historically has been and continues to be in charge of most of the doors. Holmes's family familiarity with whiteness has given her the privilege of the kind of Black person that middle-to-upper-class white people tend to feel comfortable around.

Although Holmes focuses on the fact that she has a white parent, Black and other children of color who are adopted by a white family also could have white privilege. The biological connection that Holmes has to a white parent is not what gives her access to white privilege, in other words. It is the white cultural environment that was provided by her family. No matter a person's race, the habits that constitute the self—a person's implicit styles of thinking, their typical ways of responding to situations, and so on—are fundamentally shaped by the home in which they grow up, and Holmes's self was shaped by a home that included whiteness. That same white family environment shapes the selves of children of color adopted into a home with one or more white parents. Biology isn't particularly relevant on this point.

The way that white privilege and family familiarity can impact the lives of people of color is different for different racial groups and in different nations. White privilege is never as simple as white versus Black, as the examples of Jamaica, South Africa, and Brazil show. Jamaica has three racial groups: white, Brown, and Black. Similarly, in South Africa, the three racial groups are white, Coloured, and Black, and the South African term "Coloured" is not the same thing as the outdated term "colored people" in the United States. Brown Jamaicans and Coloured South Africans are considered Black people in the United States, but they constitute a different racial group in Jamaica and South Africa. Their racial status literally changes when they step off the plane in the United States, and a similar situation holds in the very multiethnic, multiracial Brazil. And yet, in all three cases, Blackness is the negative against which other colors and races are valued. It's important to not lose sight of the particularly anti-Black nature of racism in most parts of the Western world. A racial hierarchy exists in which white people are at the top and the darkest Black people are at the bottom, with lighter-skinned non-white people in between. This hierarchy is the product of anti-Black racism. It was created by white people as part of their attempts to dominate people of color.

In the United States, even with its "one-drop" rule in which any amount of Blackness makes a person non-white, whiteness has a long history of expanding to include light-skinned members of non-white groups, such as Italians and the Irish, who have not always counted as white. It has done this to adapt and thrive in changing social conditions. For this reason, some have predicted an upcoming age of "beige supremacy" in which light-skinned Asians and Hispanics/Latinx will be granted entry to the club of white domination (Mills 2007; see also Lind 1998). But replacing white supremacy with beige supremacy would do little if anything to eliminate the fundamentals of a racial hierarchy at which Blackness is at the bottom. It would only tinker a bit at the top, allowing a few more people than before into the highest category of white-ish people.

In contrast to this view, some believe that this hierarchy recently has been flipped upside down. For example, a 2016 *Washington Post* survey

"Only white people have white privilege"

revealed that white Americans think that anti-white bias is now more prevalent than anti-Black bias (Sommers and Norton 2016). Political commentator Benjamin Shapiro argues that the result of civil rights movements and other attempts to end racism has been to place Black people at the top (Shapiro 2015). In this view, being Black now is an advantage in the United States, especially in the media, in the academy, and in politics. White privilege has been replaced by Black privilege. For Shapiro, no better proof of this alleged fact can be found than in the situation of Rachel Dolezal. A civil rights activist, Dolezal was the president of the Spokane, Washington, chapter of the National Association for the Advancement of Colored People (NAACP) in 2014–15. She resigned when her (white) parents revealed that Dolezal was white and not Black, as Dolezal had presented herself throughout adulthood. The subsequent controversy concerning Dolezal's identification as a Black woman was intense. Was this a form of fraud, a white person's effectively stealing something that didn't belong to her? Or was it a genuine and legitimate form of racial identification, demonstrating that race is socially constructed rather than biologically determined? The debate rages on, but no matter which side you take, Dolezal is still a white woman who

40

wanted to be Black. Shapiro argues that Blackness was an asset for her, giving her personal and political advantages that she would not have had if she identified as a white woman. Whether her adoption of Blackness was an act of white theft or a gesture of white respect, Dolezal valued Blackness and eagerly traded in (traded up) her whiteness for it.

What, in more detail, are the privileges that Blackness supposedly provides? Modeled on Peggy McIntosh's (1989) seminal knapsack of invisible white privileges—or, better put, parodying her[1] essay—some critics of Black privilege have provided a checklist of the advantages that Black people allegedly have over white people. (The anonymous author of the blog post identifies as an American, "not hyphenated," who has studied McIntosh's list in a university sociology class [Icanseethruyou 2012b].) The list of forty-four items includes:

- "Blacks have the right to take pride in their race. Whites don't."
- "Blacks are permitted to notice race. Whites are not."
- "Blacks have the right to riot and commit violent acts in response to perceived grievances. White people have to obey the law at all times."
- "Blacks have 'civil rights'. Whites don't."

- "Blacks have the right to support programs from the government. White people don't."
- "Blacks have the right to affirmative action and minority set-asides. Whites have to earn their positions."
- "Blacks have the right to make blacks only organizations like the Black Student Union and the Congressional Black Caucus. Whites don't."

The goal of the list is to "help them [Black people] realize what they have taken for granted and they are clearly overlooking" (Icanseethruyou 2012a).

Finally, African American radio and television personality Charlamagne Tha God brought the concept of Black privilege into the mainstream in 2017 with his book *Black Privilege: Opportunity Comes to Those Who Create It* (2017). Provocatively titled, the book encourages all his readers to embrace the idea that they are privileged. As Tha God claims, "I believe I'm just as privileged—if not more—as any white person out there" (2017, xviii–xix). A month after its publication, *Black Privilege* made it to number six on the *New York Times* list of best-selling nonfiction books.

If you read the entirety of Tha God's book, however, you'll find that his concept of Black privilege is very different from that of Shapiro. In the final chapter, "Access Your Black Privilege," Tha God clarifies, "not for a second am I suggesting that racism isn't real. It's as real as the air we breathe" (2017, 279). Everyone has privilege, according to Tha God, because each of us is unique and original. Tha God's eight-step self-help book wants each person to affirm who they are in their uniqueness. Tha God's personal version of this privileged uniqueness is Black in particular because he is "100 percent a black man" (2017, 281). Affirming that fact helps him ignore those who say that he is inferior to others. The message of Tha God's *Black Privilege* is similar to the spirit of the 1960s "Black Is Beautiful" movement, which resisted the degradation of Blackness through its affirmation. Despite his book's title, Tha God never claims that Black people have racial privileges that disadvantage white people (and people of other races).

While each of the forty-four items on the Black Privilege Checklist could benefit from discussion of who has racial privilege and what it is, what stands out in the list overall is how severely acontextual and ahistorical it is. It is as if the complex history of whiteness and class in the United States never existed. Let me focus on just one of the checklist's claims: "Blacks have the right to affirmative action and minority set-asides." Consider, for example, university scholarships that are "set aside" for African American students, Latinx/Hispanic students, and Indigenous students. I have had white people argue forcefully with me that this is a sign of both the current privilege of being non-white and the uphill battle that non-wealthy white students have to fight nowadays to get a college education. I also have been told by white people that it is unfair that Black people get to have "openly proclaimed black colleges," meaning HBCUs (Historically Black Colleges and Universities), while openly proclaimed white colleges are not allowed.

The rising costs of higher education are a real issue for non-wealthy students of all races, including white students. We should not, however, mistake that issue for Black (or other non-white) privilege. It is false, for example, that Black, Hispanic/Latinx, and Indigenous students attend college at disproportionately high rates. At one hundred leading universities in the United States, for example, Black and Hispanic/Latinx students were more underrepresented in 2017 than they were in 1980—that is, they are *more* underrepresented even after the introduction of affirmative action (Ashkenas et al. 2017). So-called set-asides implemented after the civil rights movement have not resulted in a drop in white students' admission to these universities—far from it. Widening the historical window beyond the civil rights era, recall that Black people were forbidden to attend white colleges and universities. This is why HBCUs, such as Fisk University and Howard University, were created in the 1860s. They weren't a privileged perk. They were the only way that newly freed slaves and their offspring had a chance at a higher education. In a cruelly ironic twist of history, critics of so-called Black privilege use the existence of HBCUs, minority scholarships, and other explicit measures taken to make up for the exclusion of Black people from higher education to argue that Black people have privileged access to it. Black privilege critics misconstrue efforts to secure Black people's basic rights—not just the right to education, but also fair housing, voting rights, and access to public facilities—turning them into ahistorical "evidence" that "Blacks have 'civil rights', whites don't."

The racial hierarchy of white at the top and Black at the bottom is still in place. It wasn't flipped on its head by the elimination of Jim Crow. If anything, the hierarchy seems even sturdier now that it is subtler and more implicit than in the days of open segregation and explicit discrimination. To acknowledge this grim truth is not to ignore or to disrespect the challenges to and subversions of white privilege made by Black and other people of color. Nor is it to imply that the point of recognizing white privilege is to help a few middle-to-upper-class people of color benefit from it. In particular, I want to be clear that the point of my example about the adoption of Black children by white parents is not that Black children should be reared by white families instead of Black ones. White adoption of Black children often contributes to the destruction of Black families, who could remain intact if they had housing assistance and access to adequate child care (Roberts 2002). The upshot of the examples of people of color's white and light-skinned privilege is that white privilege can cross racial lines *and* still benefit white people in the end. Some people of color might make more money and have access to power because of their white privilege, but the big winner overall remains white people as a group.

This point about the big winner is why I describe people of color with family familiarity with whiteness as "benefitting from white privilege" rather than as "experiencing less racism." I know that the claim that they experience less racism would be less controversial. But it doesn't reveal how white privilege *succeeds*, rather than fails, by occasionally giving some racial benefits to select groups of non-white people. Historically, white privilege was not weakened when it did that. It was strengthened, and this invidious pattern needs to be recognized as a particularly deceptive form of white privilege. In white-dominated countries, whiteness, especially in its middle-to-upper-class version, generally remains the normative standard by which people of all races are judged, to which we are supposed to aspire, and for which we are rewarded. The fact that some people of color are allowed to benefit from that standard hasn't dismantled it.

3

"White people should feel guilty"

Many people think that the result of white people's recognizing their white privilege should be for them to feel guilty or ashamed about it. (The issue of white guilt interestingly doesn't come up often for people of color with white privilege since their privilege generally isn't recognized.) This can take place in classrooms, reading groups, faith communities, conversations with friends and family, and many other everyday settings. The idea is that white people's guilt and shame will motivate them to take responsibility for their privilege: repent, reject, fight, and otherwise try to eliminate it. In turn, white people who don't seem to feel guilty or ashamed of their white privilege often are criticized for being racist. But are white guilt and shame really the right approach for a white person to take if they want to challenge white privilege? And what about people of color who have some white privilege? Are they also supposed to feel guilty and ashamed about the advantages that whiteness can provide them?

I acknowledge that in the short term, white guilt and shame might motivate white people to take responsibility for their white privilege. In the long run, however, I think that guilt and shame don't provide the emotional fuel to sustain the ongoing, difficult work of fighting racism and white privilege. Even worse, instead of being tools to make positive change, white guilt and shame sometimes function as postures of moral righteousness assumed by "good" white people. By publicly demonstrating that they are the good ones, they can distinguish themselves from the "bad" whites, who supposedly are the real racists. As we will see in this chapter, the line between "good" and "bad" white people drawn by many (good) white people is heavily classed. Good white people tend to be middle-to-upper-class, and they often dump responsibility for racism onto lower-class white people. This not only doesn't help the problem; it actually makes it worse. Middle-to-upper-class white people let themselves off the hook for their racism and white privilege, and lower-class white people can come to see concerns about racism and white privilege as an upper-class charade. On this scenario, the concept of white privilege looks merely like a stick that well-to-do whites use to beat poor white people. In the end, avoiding white guilt and shame when grappling with white privilege might do more to dismantle it than encouraging white people to feel guilty or ashamed.

* * *

There is a joke that circulated in 2008 right after Barack Obama was elected President of the United States: how many white people voted for Obama? Answer: A lot of guilt-ridden ones. The joke comes from a politically conservative perspective that accuses white liberals of being excited about Obama's presidency merely because it allowed them to get rid of their guilt about racism and being white. To the extent that the joke is funny, what makes it funny is that it says something true in an unexpected form. Instead of an answer like "40 percent," the supposed truth conveyed by the joke is that guilt motivated a lot of white people to vote for Obama. An Obama presidency offered a long-desired prospect of racial redemption for white people. It provided a way for them to get free of the guilt and shame that America's racist past had heaped on them. No wonder that a 2008 political cartoon from a conservative newspaper in Georgia showed Obama seeming to walk on water when in fact he was supported by submerged stepping stones labeled "white liberal guilt" (Lester 2008). The cartoon tells us that white liberals saw Obama as Jesus Christ, their savior, but that Obama wasn't really a miracle-worker. He just knew how to benefit politically from white guilt.

Does the Obama joke say something true? I don't know if white people's main motivation for voting for Obama was white guilt. I'm relatively clueless on that point. I'm also troubled by the attack on Obama's achievements contained in the joke, as if white people were responsible for Black people's accomplishments. That is a "truth" that's been told by white people since at least the seventeenth century, and we should be on the lookout for its contemporary versions. But I do know that the joke hits home in a certain way. Feeling guilty and ashamed often are assumed to be the right way for white people to react to the realization of their racial privilege. I see this not only in scholarly publications, but also in everyday life. Most of the time, white people avoid talking or even thinking about their whiteness and its advantages. When they get into a situation where they can't avoid this, however, they often don't know what to do. The fail-safe move is to make clear somehow that they don't approve of racism, and they can do so by showing that they feel guilty about it. Disastrous situation (= being perceived as racist) averted, they can return to not thinking about it.

But white guilt and shame aren't very effective. That is one reason that they are problematic from a racial justice perspective. They can make it seem like white people are doing something, but their guilt and shame don't really change anything. Another more significant reason that white guilt and shame are problematic is that they can turn white people into even bigger obstacles to racial justice than they already are. White guilt and shame might actually make the problem worse, in other words. One example of this is found in empirical evidence that white people who voted for Obama then deliberately *gave themselves permission* to favor white people over people of color (Fleming 2018, 125). Stop and reflect on that stunning fact for a moment ... Absolved of any racial guilt by voting for an African American, white people could discriminate guilt-free against people of color because they supposedly had established themselves as non-racist.

To unpack further why white guilt and shame are problematic, we need to distinguish between them. I've been using the terms "guilt" and "shame" as synonyms here, and I will continue to do so since that is how they tend to be used in everyday life. It is worth noting, however, that social scientists and other scholars who study emotions distinguish between guilt and shame. Guilt involves a specific act that a person did or did not do. If I hurt someone, for example, and realize it, I might feel guilty for my act—and then also do something to make up for my wrongdoing. Psychologists have shown that guilt can lead to beneficial change, but only if it is linked to a specific act of individual wrongdoing (Tangney 1995). Here is where white guilt runs into trouble. Many white people who benefit from white privilege haven't committed specific, explicitly racial or racist acts of individual wrongdoing. "I didn't own slaves; I have never lynched anyone; I don't use the 'n' word; I didn't choose to be born white. So in what sense am I guilty of anything?" as white people today sometimes ask. If the charge of white guilt isn't connected to a specific act, then it can sound like something made-up in order to dump on white people.

For this reason, scholars have moved away from the concept of white guilt to the concept of white shame. Shame isn't about a particular act, and so it avoids the particular problems that the concept of guilt runs into. Shame instead is about who a person is. Shame also has an explicit social dimension to it.

"White people should feel guilty"

Shame comes from being seen by others as a kind of person that I should not be. I am ashamed when I do not live up to expectations that others have for me and that I have internalized for myself. White shame thus is shame for being a white person, not guilt for what I have or haven't done to people of color. By being a white person with white privilege, I unfairly benefit from my race, and if I care about justice, I should be ashamed of that fact. My feelings of shame hopefully then will motivate me to change myself and the world so that my shame is alleviated.

The problem with shame, however, is that it doesn't typically work this way. Time and again, empirical studies demonstrate that rather than motivating people to take responsibility for a situation, shame leads them to lash out with hostility toward others, and sometimes also themselves (Tangney 1995, Scheff 2000, Velotti et al. 2016). Shame tends to be part of a shame-rage spiral in which feelings of shame lead to humiliated fury, which in turn creates more shame and then more rage and fury, and so on. Resentment, anger, blaming others, aggression, and violence – *these* are the emotions and reactions that shame tends to produce, not empathy for others and reparative actions to change an unfair situation. While these studies focus on shame in general, there is no reason to think that white shame is any different. Encouraging white people to feel ashamed of themselves for their whiteness isn't going to make them more likely to fight for racial justice. Just the opposite: it's going to make them resentfully oppose it.

It goes without saying that this is about the last thing that racial justice movements need. So why then are white guilt and shame being promoted given that they are either ineffective or downright counterproductive to racial justice movements? I think there are at least two answers to this question. First, there don't seem to be a lot of other options for white people who want to demonstrate to others that they aren't racist. I don't mean to sound snarky as I say that. It's understandable that white people often react with displays of guilt when confronted with racism and white privilege given the intense social disapproval that comes with seeming to be racist nowadays. Perhaps that disapproval even comes merely with being white. "Whiteness isn't cool [anymore], it's not on the right side of history," as Latina philosopher Linda Martín Alcoff (2015, 7) has noted, which creates an existential dilemma for white people that they are unaccustomed to. They also generally aren't prepared for it, and their lack of preparation is compounded by white fragility (white people's inability to tolerate even small amounts of racial stress; DiAngelo 2018). White people—the "good" ones, in any case—tend to be racially illiterate, not knowing how to read themselves or other white people in terms of race. White families almost never talk about race, much less whiteness in particular, for example. Teaching white children to not see race—to be racially colorblind—is supposed to inoculate them against becoming racist. The result is that white people, adults as well as children, are left with a very thin set of options for how to live their whiteness: feel guilty about it like good white people are supposed to do, or be a bad white person.

This leads to the second answer to the question of why white guilt and shame tend to be the go-to reactions for white people confronted with racism and white privilege. Displays of white guilt and shame help reinforce a class hierarchy between good white people and the bad racist ones, based on the purported moral goodness of middle-to-upper-class white people. Lower-class white people are the supposedly retrograde white people who have clung to racist beliefs. They are too stupid and/or too uneducated to have progressed with the times. They are stuck in their bigotry and backwardness, using the "n" word, for example, and generally remaining hostile to people of color. *They* are the problem; *they* are the reason that racism still exists. Good white people, in contrast, know better. They are not like the bad white people; they are not racist. They are educated and progressive. By drawing a sharp line between themselves and the bad white people, they can ensure their moral superiority and racial redemption from white people's sordid racial past.

Displays of white guilt and shame are one of the key ways to draw this sharp line. They are not politically neutral emotions. White guilt and shame operate as a kind of cultural capital for middle-to-upper-class white people. By "cultural capital," I mean an asset that is related to but different from financial resources (economic capital) and social connections/networks (social capital). Cultural capital is a kind of knowledge of a society or group, often implicit, that is embodied in attitudes, gestures, and ways of responding to situations (Preston 2009, 15). Knowing how to handle yourself appropriately in a particular culture or social situation is an asset. It helps position you well within that culture. White guilt and shame tend to be forms of cultural capital in middle-to-upper-class post-Jim Crow America. Publicly showing that you feel guilty or ashamed of your whiteness is a way of responding to racism that positions you well as a white person. It demonstrates your moral goodness; it proves that you are a good white person.

What do good white people's demonstrations of their guilt and shame look like? They often take the form of white people's talking about how bad they feel about racism. Think here of classrooms, reading groups, social movement organizations, and similar settings. This usually occurs after the concerns of people of color are made known (in person and/or via reading materials). The white person's responses of guilt and shame can be emotionally charged, sometimes in the form of a weepy outburst and almost always made in a confessional tone. For white women in particular, they tend to include becoming teary and crying. Confronting the horrific details of racism is too much for them to bear, and so they melt down emotionally. Especially when people of color are interpreted as angry or hostile when talking about racism—which they typically are interpreted as being—white women often resort to tears (Srivastava 2006). This too is white fragility in action.

When I describe this situation as a demonstration of white guilt and shame, I don't mean that it is fake. The tears and the accompanying feelings often are very real; they are not a performance or an act. For anyone, not just a white person, to realize their connection to and complicity with a vast history and present of racial injustice can be overwhelming, and white people have good reasons to feel guilty or ashamed about both their history and the present. But dramatic displays of white guilt and shame are not a cultural option equally available to poorer and working-class white people. Those displays would not provide them the cultural capital that they provide middle-to-upper-class white people. Instead, emotional displays often confirm stereotypes of poor and working-class people (including whites) being loud, unruly, and out of control. They confirm the need for their regulation since they don't know how to behave properly and control themselves (especially their bodies) in polite society. The irony here is cruel: the same emotional display of white guilt and shame that would increase a middle-class person's cultural capital would decrease that of a working-class white person.

Demonstrations of white guilt and shame don't always involve tears. They can be much subtler than an emotional meltdown. For example, when white scholars, journalists, and other critics of whiteness speak and write about white privilege, they often begin with a personal confession of their own racial privilege. This makes sense in that no one has a bias-free perspective that unerringly describes the world. It's good scholarly practice to be upfront about the context of and assumptions built into what one says. When this practice becomes an implicitly required display of white guilt and shame, however, its purpose has changed. The purpose has become a demonstration of one's moral goodness in order to accrue the cultural (intellectual) capital that comes with it.

A more overt example of white guilt that involves anger rather than tears comes from a university course that I taught in the early 2010s. It was a large lecture class of about one hundred undergraduate students, most of whom were white. There were two female teaching assistants (TAs) working with me in the class, one of whom was white and the other of whom was Black. At one point during the lecture and discussion, a white female undergraduate, "Kim" (a pseudonym), said something racially offensive to the entire class about feeling frightened of Black men if she saw one walking toward her on the sidewalk. Before anyone else could react, the white TA, "Jane" (a pseudonym), jumped up and scolded her publicly, telling Kim that what she said was racist and that she shouldn't have said it and also shouldn't feel that way. Kim responded by sitting down with an annoyed "humph" and shot back, "Oh, so only PC things can be said in this class!"

"White people should feel guilty"

This example not only illustrates a good white person in action (Jane). It also shows a white person (Kim) refusing to give in to the white guilt and shame being dumped on her. (Lest it seem like I'm picking on my TA, note that I, the main instructor, did the other typical thing that good white people do: I didn't say anything and quickly moved away from the subject to get the class back on topic for the day. More on good white people's silence about race in the next chapter.) Does Kim's refusal to be ashamed of her anti-Black comment mean that she is a bad white person? Was Kim right that Jane was trying to be politically correct and to monitor the entire class so that it was PC too?

We need to unpack the term "political correctness" before we can answer those questions. Dating back to the Russian Revolution during WWI, the term initially was used as description of a political policy, perhaps even as a compliment. Fairly quickly, however, it became a term loaded with moral and/or political judgment, criticizing something or someone perceived as imposing a rigid orthodoxy. By the late 1980s to early 1990s, "political correctness" became a hot-button issue in higher education in the United States and elsewhere when colleges and universities were criticized by conservatives for allegedly pushing left-wing ideology onto students.

"White people should feel guilty"

It remains a hot-button issue today, for example, with accusations such as "political correctness is destroying Australia's cultural heritage and what is best about our institutions . . . similar to what is happening in America, Europe, and the U.K." (Donnelly 2018). One hundred years after the birth of the term, "politically correct" inevitably is an accusation or a way of ridiculing someone. It is never a self-description. It accuses someone else of trying to censor people via shaming and other forms of social pressure, restricting what they can say or think to what is currently politically acceptable. Anything that isn't politically acceptable isn't supposed to be said or thought on penalty of being labeled politically incorrect.

When Kim accused Jane of being PC, she basically was saying that Jane (and implicitly, the rest of the white people in the class, including me) wasn't any different than Kim was when it comes to fear of Black people, especially Black men. Unpacking Kim's disgusted "humph," she likely would have said:

> If you want to call my fear of Black men racist, go ahead, but at least I am being honest about what white people think. White people like Jane have sophisticated words to make it look like they think and feel differently than the rest of us. They say

"people of color" instead of "colored people" and "Indigenous people" instead of "Native American" or "Indian," but this is just window dressing. It makes educated people like Jane look good, like they really care about racial justice. Jane also is using this to make people like me look bad. But behind these fancy words, it's no different between Jane and me. Educated, upper-crust white people aren't any less racist than the poorer, working-class ones. Their language just allows them to gloss over that fact. Political correctness is superficial and fake, hiding what people really think.

I think that Kim is wrong in saying that what language is used when talking about race—or just about anything else—is superficial. Language matters because it embodies different concepts and ideas, different ways of understanding the world. For example, it is not an exaggeration to say that different worlds are implied when calling someone "Indigenous" rather than "Native American." The term "Native American" assumes and implicitly endorses the perspective of white European settler colonialism, in which Indigenous sovereignty is a non-issue. The West supposedly has been won, the so-called Indian Wars are over, and "Native Americans" now are one racial group among others in the United States, rather than a sovereign

Indigenous people who continue to struggle for their land and right to self-governance (Rifkin 2017). The different worlds contained in language also explain why racial microaggressions are significant. "Micro" doesn't mean trivial, as some critics of the concept of microaggressions claim. "Micro" distinguishes aggressions that are not spectacularly violent (for example, a white person's calling a Black man "boy") from the ones that are (for example, white people's lynching of Black people). Both types of aggression perpetuate an anti-Black world, and both contribute to Black morbidity and mortality, albeit at different paces.

But Kim also is partially right. Language isn't enough. White people who say they are against racism and white privilege generally haven't put their money where their mouth is. I mean that both metaphorically and literally. Metaphorically, where is the substance or the action to go along with the words? Words alone, without anything else, are relatively easy. They can be used by good white people as a "get off the hook" card. As long as they use the right words, then nothing else needs to be done. Especially not anything that would involve actual money, such as making available affordable housing, adequately funded public schools, fair and livable wages, and so on. The money to back up good white people's words also is literal. Really challenging white privilege would mean concrete action against the problem of the racial inequality of wealth in the United States and other white privileged countries. (South Africa particularly comes to mind on this point.) Kim is right about the problem of good white people's hypocrisy. It's not that lower-class white people aren't racist; they sometimes, perhaps even often, are. But so are middle-to-upper-class white people, we just don't tend to see it. We are really good at recognizing racially offensive behavior and speech when it comes from white lower-class people, but we often misrecognize racially offensive behavior and speech when it comes from middle-to-upper-class white people (Preston 2009, 129).

Even though there is something to Kim's charge of political correctness, that doesn't necessarily mean that anytime white people try to learn about racial injustice, they are trying to dump white guilt on other white people. This sometimes is how the PC charge works, and the effect (whether intended or not) is to dismiss issues of racial injustice, including white people's knowledge about it. Take the example of an affluent, predominantly white Illinois high school that in 2017 devoted its annual all-day seminar for students to "Understanding Today's

Struggle for Racial Civil Rights" (New Trier High School 2017). The large array of topics included "Between Facebook and Ferguson," "Tracing Food Inequality: Food Deserts in Chicago," and "Understanding Implicit Bias: Being Biased Doesn't Make You a Bad Person." The seminar's FAQ page stated explicitly that "the purpose of the seminar was to help students better understand the history and current status of racial civil rights in the United States, not to promote the philosophy of one political party or another, or to connect a political party to the history of racial civil rights. . . . To that end, the seminar day will not portray any political party as good or bad" (New Trier High School 2017). The seminar day nonetheless was criticized by *The Weekly Standard*, a self-described conservative magazine based in Washington, D.C., for "set[ting] aside an entire day to program student minds with the shame of white privilege" and asking students to take a white privilege survey with "loaded questions to measure their guilt" (Byrne 2017).

Is that what happened at the seminar? We can't answer that question without knowing how the workshop sessions were conducted. *The Weekly Standard* describes the list of speakers as "chock-a-block with left-wing, white-guilt proselytizers" (Byrne 2017). (Recall the joke about Obama's election and note the conflation of "left-wing" and "white guilt" here, as if you can't be or have one without the other.) And for all I know, the seminar sessions were conducted in a way that merely shamed the white students who attended. But maybe not. The mere fact of these particular topics being discussed does not mean that the purpose or the effect of the workshop was to make white students feel ashamed of their race. When we assume that any non-racially offensive talk of race by white people has no other purpose than to guilt and shame white people, then we have dismissed the reality of racism and white privilege and the need to learn about them.

Finally, it is striking that questions about white guilt and shame rarely, if ever, come up for Black, Latinx/Hispanic, and other people of color with some white privilege. In large part, of course, that probably is because we assume that only white people can have white privilege. But I think it is also because fights about white guilt primarily are an intra-white battle. They take place between white people. Here's an interesting fact: it generally is not Black people and other people of color who are calling for white people to feel guilty or criticizing white people for allegedly being PC and trying to shame other white people. Rather than watch white people wallow in racial guilt, most people of color would prefer that they get up and do something about the problem. White people do have things to be ashamed about because of their race. But too often, white guilt and shame become an excuse for ignorance about racism and white privilege and a substitute for anger and action against them (Lorde 1984). It is white people who tend to overly focus on white guilt when they learn about racism and white privilege—that is, if they don't react with hostility and resentment—and it's unclear that doing so does anything to address or to eliminate them. In fact, more often than not, white guilt gets in the way. It becomes a red herring that sidetracks white people from the real issue. It would be better in most cases for white people and others with white privilege to sidestep it, rather than become sidetracked by it. They then might be able to figure out a way to take responsibility for white privilege.

4

"White people should figure out how to get rid of their white privilege"

If white privilege is unfair, then the point of recognizing it would seem to be to eliminate it. After recognizing that you have white privilege, wouldn't it be racist to embrace it? While the answer is "yes," a better response is to refuse the question since it presents a false dilemma: get rid of your white privilege, or you have chosen to affirm racism and white superiority. The problem is that white privilege often cannot be easily discarded. It is largely structural, social, and thus independent of an individual's deliberate will and choice, even as it benefits white people in very personal, individual ways. A white person's thinking that they can or that they have eliminated their white privilege is something of a fiction, often fabricated by a desire to distance themselves from their whiteness and erase the presence of race in their lives. Being able to choose when and how one's race matters is itself another form of white privilege, after all. Most people of color do not have this luxury.

Rather than embrace their white privilege *or* think that they control how to get rid of it, white people can attempt to use white privilege against itself. This might sound paradoxical, and it almost certainly will put white people in an uncomfortable position that could jeopardize their personal, social, and professional relationships, especially with other white people. I cannot emphasize that last point enough, and I will return to it below. Paradoxical and existentially risky though it might be, however, white people can use their position as white people to jam a stick in the wheels of white privilege. White people have access to the many de facto white-only spaces that still exist, for example, and they can use their presence, words, and action in those spaces to disrupt the patterns of white privilege that shape them.

* * *

If you have white privilege and could do something to get rid of it, what would it be? Since the end of Jim Crow, white people's typical answer to this question—when they think about it at all—has been racial colorblindness. "I don't see race, I just see people," is the idea behind colorblindness. White people's colorblindness can be thought of as a kind of white silence. Don't see race, don't talk about race, and then it can't do any harm. In contrast, talking about race can seem (especially to white people) to magnify its presence and all the problems that it entails. The right thing to do, the polite thing to do, is to try to see people as raceless. On this line of thinking, only rude (= racist) white people notice another person (of color)'s race.

White people use the strategy of racial color-blindness all the time, even if they don't call it by that name. Sometimes they attempt to be color-blind to avoid the topic of white privilege, rather than to eliminate it, but either way, the appeal of colorblindness is strong. As I mentioned in Chapter 3, this is especially true in the context of rearing white children. Even when highly visible events, such as the fatal police shooting of Michael Brown in Ferguson, Missouri, spark intense racial protest and thus would seem to require talking about race, white parents tend to stay silent (Underhill 2017). If very young white kids have no idea what race and racial privilege are, isn't it best to leave things that way? Won't talking with children about race and the alleged superiority of white people put ideas in their mind about white privilege that they otherwise wouldn't have had? White colorblindness and white silence can seem like the best ways to prevent that from happening and thus to get rid of white privilege.

White colorblindness and white silence also are appealing to many white people since they often don't know what to do when the topic of race pops up. Recall the way that I handled the situation when my white teaching assistant, Jane, publicly shamed my white undergraduate student, Kim, for saying something racist in class. I froze up for a second, panicking internally, and then awkwardly moved the class on to the material that we were supposed to be discussing. Perhaps my immediate silence about what happened in class is somewhat understandable since I was on the spot. The whole thing happened very fast, and there was no time to reflect on the best way to undo Jane's shaming of Kim without either excusing Kim's racist comment or shaming Jane in turn. That is a tricky combination to pull off no matter how much time one has to brainstorm what to say. For me, at least, it was impossible to do in the heat of the moment.

But I *did* have ample time between class on Monday and the next class on Wednesday. I could have come into class on Wednesday and tried to lead a discussion about white women's fear of

Black men in a way that listened to Kim, rather than scolding her, but also without letting what she said stand unexamined. I don't pretend to know the perfect way to have that conversation with a roomful of mostly, but not exclusively, white people. Was there a way to take up Kim's remark without harming the people of color in the room? Was there a way to do it that wouldn't come off as pressure from the teacher to be politically correct? In any case, I'll never know. On Wednesday, I ran the class like any other class, not saying a thing about what happened on Monday. What was the result? It was not that issues of race and beliefs in white superiority disappeared from the classroom. It was that everyone clammed up about them, unwilling to risk talking about race. I bet that half the white women in the room felt the same way that Kim did about Black men but weren't brave enough—it was a kind of bravery, after all, even if problematic—to say it out loud. My silence didn't change that. It allowed those beliefs to stay put.

White silence and white colorblindness are a sham. I don't mean that white people are silent about and "blind" to race in order to intentionally dupe people of color. I mean instead that white silence and white colorblindness promise something that they cannot deliver. They generally do not help reduce or eliminate white privilege. They are perfectly consistent with anti-Black racism, for example, while offering virtually no resources for combating it. They allow white privilege to hum along under the surface, unchallenged and unde-tected (by white people, at least). One of the most vivid examples of this comes from a recent study of white suburban parents in California (Lewis 2003). In interviews about their views on race, white par-ents often expressed their beliefs that they didn't care what another person's race was, that all people should be colorblind, and that they were teaching their children to be colorblind as good parents should. In later moments of the interviews, how-ever, when white parents were asked if they would be okay if their white daughter married someone from a different race, their responses were reveal-ing. As one white mother explained,

> It depends what race . . . I do, to me, Asians aren't—to me it is, I hate to say this, it sounds so prejudiced, but to me it's more like blacks are, African-Americans would be the only . . . to me Asians are just like—white. And I guess I am just realizing I am saying that (laughs). . . . But I wouldn't feel um, uncomfortable at all if my daughter, you know, married a, an Asian person or I wouldn't have felt strange dating an Asian person in college,

but I would have felt a little bit—I would have felt
uncomfortable dating a black man. (2003, 160)

After halting, stammering, and half-speaking her
discomfort about Black people, the woman finally
blurted out her preference for Asians because they
are the racial minority most like white people. She
wasn't unique; many other white people interviewed
as part of the study expressed similar contradictory
feelings. Even though in theory racial colorblindness
conflicts with beliefs in the superiority of whiteness,
in practice the two can and often do coexist quite
easily.

If white colorblindness and white silence aren't
good responses to the question of how to get rid
of white privilege, what are some better answers?
Details and context matter, both for what one
might do and for whether that act would succeed
in eliminating racial and/or race-class privilege. To
get a handle on this, let's return to the examples of
white privilege from Chapter 1: (1) a white person's
getting a warning instead of a ticket for speeding, (2) a white person's being allowed to take a
slightly oversized carry-on bag on the plane, and
(3) a white person's being allowed to rent a house
without providing a security deposit. What would it
look like—in real life, not just in theory—for white

people to give up their white (class) privilege in those situations?

In the speeding example, notice that this question assumes that I was aware at the time that my race-class privilege was a significant factor in the situation. This is a somewhat large assumption given my adrenalin-boosted heart rate and my laser-beam focus on making sure that I didn't startle the police officer when I reached for my auto registration and driver's license. It also is a large assumption given how quickly everything happened at the end of the encounter, when the officer let me go with a warning. Until that point, I was certain I was going to get the ticket that I deserved. At the last minute, he changed his mind, told me to slow down, and within two seconds he was back at his own car. It was at this moment, after it was too late, that I realized that my white class privilege likely was what got me off the hook.

"After it was too late" ... too late to do what, exactly? What could or should I have done if I had realized in the heat of the moment that my white class privilege was in play? Or failing that, if I had gotten out of my car to talk with the officer as he walked back to his vehicle? I don't intend those questions defensively, as in "Gimme a break, what could I have done?!" (And I admit that I was relieved to get a warning instead of an expensive ticket and a required court appearance.) Instead I'm trying to imagine concretely what can be done to turn down white class privilege when it is granted to (forced upon) you. Should I have asked the officer to give me a ticket? Explained to him that I thought he was being unfair in letting me go with a warning just because I was white and middle-class? Asked him not to let racial and class biases toward people like me affect his discretion in when to issue tickets? Asked him also to let people of color and poor people go with a warning when he stopped one of them? I am hard pressed to imagine what the officer might have done if I had said these things. Perhaps he would have given me a ticket. My worry is that he instead would have arrested me for "contempt of cop," aka, disorderly conduct or obstructing a police officer. But even if he just looked at me oddly, shrugged, and wrote out the ticket, I would not have eliminated my white class privilege. I just would have exercised it in a different form. I would have been allowed to do something off-script and gotten away with it—seen as "eccentric," not arrested, and no gun pulled on me—precisely because of my white class privilege (combined with my gender, I would add).

The second case, involving the carry-on bag at

the airport, is similar. Melinda's husband didn't realize how white class privilege affected his travel experience until a week later, when he heard what happened to his wife. Having realized it, we could ask what he ought to do if he or other white people have a similar experience in the future. As in the first example, he could tell the authority figure in question—the gate attendant, in this case—not to do it: not to allow him on the plane if she thought his bag was oversized or to please allow people of color with similar-sized bags also to take them on the plane, and so on. And the gate attendant might or might not do those things. Either way, however, Melinda's husband would not have eliminated his white class privilege. He would have been using it to challenge the gate attendants as they exercised discretion in their job.

The third case, involving the rental house, is more complicated, and perhaps for that reason it's more fruitful for thinking about whether and how white privilege could be given up. If Bill and Marie knew at the time of renting the house that the landlord was applying different rental criteria based on race, they could have refused to sign the lease and looked elsewhere for housing. If they didn't know about the different criteria before signing the lease, they could give up their white privilege by moving out of the house. (Presumably they would have to wait until their one-year lease was up or they would owe significant money for breaking the lease. An argument could be made, however, that they shouldn't remain in the house once they knew about the conditions of its rental.) Either way, by not renting the house, Bill and Marie would be relinquishing some of their racial advantages for securing housing. They would still be exercising some white privilege by choosing when and how to confront their race, but they would be doing so in a way that refuses to benefit as much from their privilege.

So, would you do it?

Before digging into this question, it's worth noting that not all examples of using white privilege against itself are as significant as Bill and Marie's situation. In fact, a lot of them are completely consistent with being a good white person who (perhaps unconsciously) cares more about being perceived as not-racist than about landing a significant blow against white privilege. Many instances of charity fall into this category. *If* they can be called situations in which white privilege is used against itself, it is only in the most cursory way. For example, in February 2018, a food truck selling Nigerian food in New Orleans asked white people to consider paying $30 for a meal that costs $12 (Godoy

2018). The 250 percent difference is consistent with the racial inequalities of wealth in the city, and the extra money went to minority customers at the food stall. About 80 percent of the white customers agreed to pay the extra money. Likewise, in 2018, a Gofundme online charity account was set up where white people who received traffic warnings could donate the amount of the ticket that they didn't receive. (People like me!) The funds raised went to The Bail Project, Inc., a California nonprofit organization that helps pay the cash bails of people who are held in jail solely because they cannot afford bail.

I wouldn't say that charitable actions on the part of white people are a sham in the way that white colorblindness and white silence are, but they are deceptive nonetheless. In the guise of helping other people, they don't really use white privilege against itself. In fact, they can strengthen white privilege, particularly its psychological and emotional sides. White charity enables white people to feel good about themselves for doing something against racism. It's a pleasure laced with class privilege to boot. Paying $18 extra for lunch or donating $150 to a charity that helps provide bail would be impossible for most poor white people, even as the extra money would hardly be missed by many middle-to-upper-class white people. I am not arguing that you should never give away money to those in need. What I am claiming is that using white privilege against itself should not be reduced to charitable giving. To really use white privilege against itself isn't going to feel good most of the time. In fact, it's probably going to be painful.

Which brings us back to Bill and Marie. Would you do it? Would you refuse to rent the house because of the unjust racial criteria used by the landlord?

It's easy to criticize Bill and Marie when you think of the Black family who was denied housing and perhaps became homeless. How could you live happily in the house knowing what you know? Let's get real here, however, and not dump too quickly on Bill and Marie. If you were facing an immediate crisis of moving into a dilapidated, overpriced apartment, at best—overpriced because no security deposit was required—and possible homelessness, at worst, would you walk away from renting the house? You might reply that maybe Bill and Marie had other options that they hadn't explored. Perhaps there were family members, for example, who could help them out until they got back on their feet again. Or maybe someone else in the church could help. Those are fair points. It's impossible to know what would have happened or how bad things could have gotten if they had refused to rent this particular house. However, you have to add to the immediate crisis the longer-term social ramifications of your not signing or breaking the lease, the friendships and community/church relationships that would be strained or broken when you explained to the landlord and others why you refused the rental house. Even if you didn't have an altercation with the landlord when walking away from the lease, you likely will be perceived by him and others as judging him to be racist. In that case, you probably couldn't count on other church members or businesspeople putting their own social relationships at stake by taking your side and giving you a helping hand. Not just housing, but Bill and Marie's community ties and Bill's new job also would dry up. Bill and Marie might very well deserve condemnation, but let's not judge them for making a decision that supposedly no other "good" white person would make. Many white people would have done the exact same thing, with more or less reluctance: rent the house, even knowing the landlord's unfair rental criteria, and accept a job from him to boot.

Revisiting these three examples reveals a few things about the idea of getting rid of white privilege. To begin, given the difficulty—sometimes the practical impossibility—of getting rid of white privilege, a better strategy is to look for ways to use it against itself. This admittedly can seem like a confusing suggestion. How can you use something and simultaneously get rid of it? It also is a strategy that will make white people feel uncomfortable. How can you know that using your white privilege isn't just strengthening it? Won't it look bad, like you are a racist white person, if you use your white privilege? The answer to these questions isn't clearcut. It all depends how and to what ends you use white privilege, and there is no guarantee that your use of white privilege will weaken it.

To unpack this a bit, consider how many predominantly white spaces there are in the United States and other countries with white privilege. Legalized segregation might not exist any longer, but de facto segregation is just as strong, if not stronger than ever. Residential neighborhoods, schools, homes, businesses, clubs, and churches and other faith-based institutions—these are social and geographical spaces that often are informally segregated by race, combined with class. This means that there are a lot of places that privilege white people by providing them "membership" in those places, including the sense of belonging that this membership provides. White people can use that privilege against itself to interrupt the whiteness of those spaces.

This doesn't have to be as dramatic as what Anne and Carl Braden did in 1954. The Bradens were a white couple living in Louisville, Kentucky, who bought a house in a white neighborhood in order to deed it to a Black couple, Charlotte and Andrew Wade. The Wades had not been able to purchase a house in the neighborhood because of a tacit agreement among the white neighbors to sell their homes only to other white people (Braden 1999). The Bradens used their privilege as middle-class white people expressly to disrupt and dismantle that privilege, and their actions still serve as a powerful example today. What civil rights leader Julian Bond claimed in 1999 continues to be true twenty years later: "What's missing today isn't Wades who want a home, but Bradens who will help them fight for one" (in Braden 1999, xii).

But there also are more mundane ways for white people to disrupt white privileged spaces, especially by refusing white silence and white colorblindness. A white person's speaking up about race and speaking against racism and white superiority in everyday situations can use white privilege against itself. When a racially offensive joke is told at a predominantly white social gathering or business meeting, for example, who will laugh awkwardly and change the subject, and who instead will say something to challenge the joke's racism? In situations where only white people are present when the joke is told, it will have to be a white person that says something—if anything is ever said. Here is where racial justice movements need white people to step up and use their access to white spaces to interrupt them.

Another everyday way for white people to interrupt white spaces is merely to notice and talk about them. This works even—or perhaps, especially—when nothing "racial" seems to have happened. Susan Raffo (2009) provides a helpful example of this. When out running errands, she and her young daughter, both of whom are white, developed a habit of actively noticing who was in the stores and shops. When they entered a café for lunch, for example, they noticed that only white people were there and they began to discuss that fact. If the white clientele was mainly local, then what did that mean about the neighborhood? Would people of color feel comfortable going to the café? Would they even know about the coffee shop and/or have easy access to it? What's really interesting about Raffo's conversation with her daughter is that they discussed how easy it was for them to fit into the atmosphere of the café. They talked about how they barely noticed that they were white when they were there. While they chose to notice their whiteness and the whiteness of the social space of the café, they had that choice—that too is white privilege, a choice that many people of color do not have. Raffo and her daughter made the whiteness of the space and of their lives visible, interrupting the "normal" way that whiteness and white privilege hide themselves.

Even though it's mundane, this interruption can be unsettling. Raffo doesn't say, but imagine that she and her daughter talked audibly about the whiteness of the café while they were there. I find myself wondering how the white staff and other white patrons reacted. Maybe the other white people ignored them. Maybe some were amused. Maybe some wanted to join the conversation. But maybe some were offended. Perhaps the offended white people said something insulting to Raffo and her daughter, making them feel unwelcome in the café. I can imagine all those scenarios happening, especially the ones in which the other white people were uncomfortable or even hostile toward Raffo. When you expose whiteness and white privilege, there is no guarantee how you will be perceived, and there is a good chance that you won't be received warmly. This is something that people of color have long known. This is something for white people to be prepared for.

The Bradens quickly found this out. When they deeded the house to the Wades, they expected that some white people would object to what they did, but they didn't think of their act as monumental. They weren't doing anything illegal, after all. Almost immediately after they transferred the house to the Wades, however, the Bradens were inundated with threatening phone calls and bomb threats. A cross was burned next to the Wades' new home, and it later was bombed. Instead of the support that the Bradens thought they would receive from white liberals in Louisville, they were criticized and ostracized. Carl was fired from his job, charged with and convicted of sedition, and spent eight months in prison before his conviction was reversed. (The Bradens' act was depicted as a communist conspiracy, a common tactic used against integrationist efforts during the McCarthy era in the United States.) Anne also was put in jail for a week and subsequently suffered a miscarriage. Far from being admired for what they had done to undermine white privilege, the Bradens were terrorized and traumatized for doing it.

Again, the Bradens' experience was remarkable,

and mundane challenges to racism in workplaces, homes, and social clubs aren't likely to result in bombings and sedition charges. And yet, we should not underestimate how emotionally and socially (as well as financially) difficult it can be to challenge white privilege, even when using it against itself. One thing about Bill and Marie's situation is for sure: if they had refused to rent the house, they would have found out very quickly the extent to which their social and business relationships with other white people were implicitly built on staying silent about—and maybe even affirming—the status quo of white privilege. They probably wouldn't have received threatening anonymous phone calls if they spoke up about the unjust rental conditions—or would they?—but I bet they still would be surprised by the responses they received, and not in a pleasant way. Likewise, to deliberately make visible the everyday whiteness of a social space, as Susan Raffo did, can result in sharp criticism and ostracism from other white people. You likely will be accused of artificially forcing race into a situation where it wasn't there, as if a space filled with white people wasn't racialized by their whiteness. ("How is race relevant in an academic department meeting when all the faculty are white?" as a white philosopher scornfully asked me a few years ago.) You will find out quickly the penalties, mundane or otherwise, for refusing white colorblindness.

It can be comforting for a white person to think that this wouldn't happen to them, that their own relationships with other white friends, family members, and colleagues are different, better, more solid. This also can be comforting for people of color with white privilege to believe. It can be reassuring to think, for example, that Bill and Marie were unfortunate in that their friendships and other relationships were buttressed by white privilege in ways that other people's friendships and relationships (yours?) are not. Whatever your race, it is comforting to think that you could never be faced with a choice between acquiescing to white privilege and losing friends and other social connections. In thinking that, you almost certainly would be wrong. While I can't prove that hunch, I invite you to test it out in your own life.

But why would you do that? Really. That is a genuine question, not a throwaway. I certainly haven't painted a very attractive picture of what challenging white privilege looks like. Frankly, it can look pretty dismal—to me, too. What would motivate a person with white (class) privilege to jeopardize their relationships in this way and to risk any financial security they might have? Why would a person subject themselves to a potential existential earthquake, with immediate tremors and unexpected aftershocks across all zones of their life, if they did not have to? The only honest answer I can think of is not based on helping other people. As I'll argue next, it has to be based on helping yourself.

5

"White people should figure out how to help people of color"

Why would a person with white (class) privilege give it up or use it against itself, especially if doing so will be painful? To help people of color? That would seem to be the most logical and also the most ethical answer. If white people generally are advantaged by their race, then it would seem to follow that people of color generally are disadvantaged by their own. If white people tend to have easier or greater access to forms of power because of their race, then people of color would seem to be relatively disempowered because of their race. In that case, shouldn't white people figure out how to help people of color so that the lives of people of color are improved? Put another way, shouldn't white people use their race-class privilege to create a fairer world? Isn't that the right thing to do after realizing that one is privileged? Helping people of color in the pursuit of racial justice—surely that explains why white people would take on the hard task of working against white privilege.

It sounds good, but it often doesn't work that way. In this final chapter, I'll debunk the idea that helping people of color works well to motivate white people to challenge their white privilege. I'll propose a different type of motivation, one that might make white people look "selfish" but that has a far greater chance of being effective. White people need to bring far more self-interest to the table of racial justice than they usually do. They need to decide whether they want to recognize that they have skin in the game of eliminating white privilege. Only in that way do they have a chance of being helpful partners of people of color in racial justice struggles.

* * *

The idea of white people using their racial privilege to help people of color is implicitly built on white people's good will. By "good will," I mean that moral ideals guide what a person cares about, wants, and does. A person with good will tries to "do the right thing" even—perhaps especially—if doing so doesn't personally benefit her. Above all, a person with good will is not selfish. She sets her own individual interests aside so that she acts according to moral values of goodness, righteousness, and justice. A person might do this for religious reasons, as part of a Christian moral commitment, for example. You could think here of the seven traditional Christian virtues and their opposites, the seven deadly sins. But being religious isn't necessary for a person to have good will. Commitment to moral ideals such as goodness and justice can be secular, held by agnostics and atheists as well.

So, what possibly could be wrong with white people's good will regarding people of color? To begin, white people's attempts to help people of color often are an unconscious exercise of white domination and condescension in disguise. If you are a white person, you probably just reacted pretty strongly to that claim, but bear with me. When good will takes the form of charitable action, the people being helped might get a little bit of benefit—some money, some access to social services, and so on— but the overall structural problems that created the inequalities and need for help aren't addressed. Instead, even if unintended, the main outcome of the charitable act tends to be the reinforcement of a centuries-old pattern: white people are positioned as generous benefactors to people of color, who in turn are supposed to gratefully receive what has been given to them. As W. E. B. Du Bois noted over one hundred years ago, if people of color ever challenge this hierarchy or are ungrateful for what they receive, "then the spell is suddenly broken" (Du Bois 1999, 19). The feel-good moment of helping others is over. White people tend to get annoyed or even angry in these situations, and at that moment, the real (unconscious) purpose of charity is revealed. Of course, white people don't typically think of themselves as dominating people of color by "helping" them. In fact, it's important to white people's sense of moral goodness that they don't consciously feel or see themselves this way. The will isn't good if its "generous" acts are motivated by condescension and a desire to keep inequalities in place. Whenever you see white people disgruntled because of the insufficient gratitude of those they have helped, however, you are seeing the white good will exposed as a cover for something else.

A second problem with relying on white people's good will toward people of color is related to the first. It's not just that selflessly helping other people often is unconsciously motivated by a desire to feel higher or better than other people. It's also that selflessly working to help others almost never provides enough fuel to keep a person going in a long, tedious struggle to achieve something, be that racial justice or anything else. Maybe Mother Theresa could keep up the energy for a brutal, seemingly endless fight to help people who were outcast and oppressed, but her exception proves the rule. Most people will run out of energy and/or interest. Maybe they will do something helpful a couple of times—give some money to the NAACP, provide a few days of physical labor to Habitat for Humanity, and so on—but then they tend to drift away from the ongoing, relentless nature of the problems. I will return below to the question of what could serve as adequate fuel for white people's ongoing work against racism and white privilege.

Since relying on white people's good will is unfruitful, and sometimes even counterproductive, let's shift the claim that "white people should figure out how to help people of color" to a more political register. By "political register," I don't mean what political party you belong to. I mean thinking about this claim at the level of the *polis*, the governed society in which you live. Political and moral commitments can overlap, of course. The important distinction between them, however, is that a moral commitment addresses individual needs while a political commitment addresses structural issues in public policy, law, education, and other social institutions.

Consider, for example, the importance of safe, drinkable water for human life. Flint, Michigan, is a predominantly African American city in the United States whose water supply is contaminated with lead. This happened because in 2014 state officials changed Flint's water source to a cheaper option and did not properly treat the water, which caused lead from the city's aging pipes to leach into the system (Clark 2018). A moral commitment to ensuring safe water to Flint residents could be enacted by helping deliver bottles of water to families in Flint. This is important as a short-term fix, but it doesn't tackle the problem that created the disaster in the first place. A political commitment to ensuring safe drinking water, in contrast, could be enacted by working to change state policies and laws that regulate water treatment facilities. Those changes would need to address the fact that government officials dismissed complaints from the mostly poor and African American residents of Flint concerning the foul-smelling water. They also would need to address the cover-up that occurred after the problem was identified, which was possible because African American lives were seen as less important than the money that the state saved. As this example shows, there are ways for white people to help people of color that are not moral acts of charity or philanthropy. They primarily are political actions generated by a commitment to justice and equality. While immediate individual needs shouldn't be ignored, political action aims to get at root causes of racial injustice and social inequality that create those needs in the first place. In that way, a more political understanding of "helping others" avoids some of the problems that a moral understanding of it does.

But political notions of racial justice and equality also can be a trap for white people. This is especially true when they remain abstract ideals. With nothing concrete to back them, lofty-sounding words can be a cover for inaction or, even worse, for harming others. As a piece of African American folk wisdom warns, when white people say "Justice," they mean "Just us" (Mills 1998). In the name of impartial fairness, white people historically have done a lot of greedy things that harm people of color. There are almost too many examples to provide one here, but think of the United States' wars against Indigenous people in North America, especially in the nineteenth century. Those wars were waged "justly" because the government was protecting its white citizens from attacks by Indigenous people, but the attacks happened primarily because white settlers had moved onto land granted by treaty to Indigenous tribes. The warning contained in African American folk aphorism doesn't just apply to African Americans. It also applies to other non-white people. It even can be heard as a warning for white people to heed. When you think you are acting in the name of justice, be careful that you aren't deceiving yourself and acting maliciously for "just us."

Here's another illustration of how ideals of justice and equality can be harmful when they are separated from concrete contexts, historical situations, and personal motivations. The rules of a society can be fair while simultaneously the entire "game" of life is not. Compare life to a game of Monopoly in which the same rules apply to all players (Jost et al. 2005). Everyone gets the same amount of money when they start playing; everyone gets $200 when they pass "Go"; everyone can buy property for the listed price when they land on it; everyone can charge rent when other players land on their property; everyone goes to jail when they land on the "Go to Jail" square; and so on. Now, imagine that some players are allowed to begin playing the game at the same time while others have to wait two, three, or more rounds before they can begin playing. You know what happens next: it doesn't matter that the same rules apply to all players working their way around the board. The players who began two or more rounds after the others are destined to lose the game. A lot of the property on the board already will have been purchased once they get to it, and they will be paying rent when they land on it. They will only be a little bit behind at first, but they will quickly slip further and further behind as each round goes by. If you walked up to the ongoing game and didn't know that some players weren't allowed to start at the same time, you might think that the losing players were less skilled or made stupid decisions when playing the game. Or maybe you would think that they had bad luck when rolling the dice. In any case, you wouldn't know that the game was rigged to favor the earlier players. Appealing to the fairness of the game's rules wouldn't address that problem. In fact, it just covers it up.

Now, imagine that the first group that began the game consisted of white middle-to-upper-class people, and that poor white people, people of color, and especially African American people had to wait a round or more to start. All the real-life rules concerning voting rights, property owner-ship, equal wages and job opportunities, and so on could be the same, but real life would still unfairly benefit middle-to-upper-class white people. The Monopoly game is only a metaphor, of course, and so it won't fit real life in all its complexity. For one thing, African American people weren't just denied the opportunity to own property for hundreds of years; they *were* the property. For another, not all the current real-life rules in the United States and other countries are the same for everyone regardless of race. But the Monopoly metaphor still shows how thin versions of justice, equality, and fairness can exist in a deeply unjust world. Deeply concrete justice, as we might call it, would have to deal with the nitty-gritty details of history and how history continues to live on today.

Finally, abstract notions of justice and equality are problematic because they generally do not provide enough fuel to keep white people interested in and committed to eliminating white privilege. As Anne Braden, the white woman in Kentucky who sold her house to a Black family in the 1950s, acknowledged, "even the most crusading of us have a tendency to vacillate and hesitate, to try to live as long as possible with the status quo, if there is nothing but abstract principle pushing us on" (Braden 1999, 11). It doesn't matter how lofty the principle is; a lofty principle alone is too gauzy to do the job. It is like a cloud: it looks like something substantial, but if you reached out to try to grab it, you'd be left empty-handed. There wouldn't be anything to take hold of. There isn't anything solid there to sustain you, push you, or help you stick with a commitment when the going gets rough. (And it will get rough.) This helps explain why some Black activists in the 1960s worried about trusting white people as allies in U.S. civil rights struggles against Jim Crow laws. It's not that the Black activists thought that the white people who joined in helping to pass the civil rights bills concerning fair housing and equal education were malicious. The white people were well-intentioned and they cared about justice, but they also were unreliable. They could and did walk away from the struggle, whenever they wanted to or whenever it got really tough, without any negative repercussions. White people were (and are) in a very different position than Black people concerning how much what they were fighting for meant in their lives (Ture and Hamilton 1992).

I think that it's possible for white people and people of color to work together to eliminate racism and white privilege. White good will, whether moral or political, does not exhaust the possibilities of white people's relationships with people of color. But we should never underestimate the capacity of white people, perhaps unconsciously, to surreptitiously use interracial cooperation as a vehicle for improving their social and cultural capital. We

101

also should never underestimate the ability of white people to literally or metaphorically move into the spaces of people of color—neighborhoods, churches, music, and so on—allegedly out of appreciation or a desire to help, but ultimately to benefit from them (Sullivan 2006). If whiteness isn't cool anymore, then white people's working side-by-side with people of color is. And so, precisely for that reason, sometimes doing the uncool thing of *not* moving into a non-white space is the best thing that a white person can do. Sometimes figuring out how to work on white privilege within white spaces is the best way for white people to take responsibility for their whiteness.

So, what might motivate a white person to do that and, moreover, to stick with the fight? The only honest answer that I can come up with is a version of self-interest. The fight has got to matter, really matter, to a white person in a concrete, personal way that they recognize. We might say that a white person has got to have some skin in the game (Alcoff 2016). It will be different skin—different things at stake—than people of color have, but it nonetheless will have to matter significantly to them. It will have to literally hurt if they lose what they have at stake in the fight, if the fight is not successful, if racism and white privilege aren't eliminated, or at least beaten back some. Not an abstract, generic kind of hurt, but real pain: emotional, psychological, physical, interpersonal. It's not that white people's pain makes white privilege disappear. Their pain isn't causal in that way. What I mean instead is that white people's experience of pain because of white privilege—if and when it is felt—is both a byproduct of and a motivation for their struggle, an indication that they know they have skin in the game, that their commitment to racial justice and equality isn't merely a convenient ideal that makes them look good, that they experience white privilege as dehumanizing *for them too*, not just for people of color.

So, where is your skin in the game, whatever your race? What would that mean in your case? How would you suffer from dehumanization if white privilege were *not* eliminated? I think that most people of color can answer these questions prettily easily, but they tend to be odd-sounding to white people. What is true of one white woman working in the 1960s African American civil rights organization CORE (Congress of Racial Equality) is probably true of many white racial justice activists: "She had long imagined herself rebelliously working against her own interests in the struggle for others' freedom. She had no idea what it meant to consider her own" (Sonnie and Tracy 2011, 20). If you are a white person, how would you answer the question of what your interests in racial justice are? I mean *really* answer it. There's no one-size-fits-all answer. The only legitimate response has got to be what really matters *to you*, and that response must be formed out of the specific details and concerns of your individual life.

It is at this moment—on this topic and at the end of the book—that you probably are wanting some clear-cut answers, especially if you are a white person. And it is here that I must remind you that this is not a feel-good book. I cannot tell you how to recognize that your skin is in the game. I can provide examples of how other white people have answered questions about their commitment to racial justice, but they inevitably will be insufficient. Anne Braden, for example, describes herself as having "an almost neurotic compulsion" to fight racial segregation in the 1950s and a paradoxical feeling of freedom when she learned emotionally, not just intellectually, that African American people were not objects to fit into white people's plans (even those of racial justice activists) or lower beings who needed her help (1999, 32). In their canonical book *Black Power*, Kwame Ture (formerly Stokely Carmichael) and Charles Hamilton also talk about a kind of freedom that has been unattainable for many white people, freedom from "subtle paternalism bred into them by the society" (Ture and Hamilton 1992, 28). Likewise, historians of poor and working-class white people who participated in the 1960s civil rights movement explain that "these men and women understood that ending racism was not a threat or an act of charity, but part of gaining their own freedom" (Sonnie and Tracy 2011, 5). As these examples suggest, white people might have skin in the game of racial justice because their own freedom is at stake.

But these examples still don't really show you how to answer the question for yourself. Freedom is a very lofty ideal, after all, and it has an especially strong appeal in the United States ("the land of the free"). Even though self-interest in freedom motivated Anne Braden, pursuit of her freedom doesn't really explain why she did what she did. What does "freedom" concretely mean, especially in the case of white people? There were lots of white people in the 1950s (like today) who strongly valued freedom in some fashion but wouldn't do what Anne and her husband did. In fact, they were some of the very people who harassed and terrorized the Bradens for their act. Why one white person sees their skin in the game and another one does not cannot be easily explained or forecast. There is no set of just the right ideals—freedom, a political passion for justice, love for family or country, et cetera—that will provide fail-safe instructions for how to feel your own skin in the game. You have to figure that out for yourself.

And let's be honest: many white people do not know how to feel that their skin is in the game. It's not something that most white people get a lot of practice doing in white communities. It's not something that "good" white families talk about as white kids are growing up, for example. It's also not an intellectual decision or a matter of having enough will power, as if you could just declare "I will care about racial justice!" and *voila*, you see how your skin is in the game. It instead is emotional and existential (what kind of agony in your life will result if this fight is not won?) and simultaneously structural (where in the game is your skin at stake?). It also is likely to occur under the pressure of an urgent, concrete experience. As Anne Braden observed, "it is only under the impact of action that human hearts and minds are ever altered anyway—only when some practical situation presents the necessity to think and feel in new ways" (Braden 1999, 289).

I think that most—all?—white people have at

least some skin in the game but don't realize it. They don't recognize how racial injustice corrodes and dehumanizes them because a white privileged world makes it difficult to see and because white people generally have a lot of defense mechanisms to "protect" them from seeing it. Some of those defense mechanisms include the erasure of Black suffering. For example, in the United States, nineteenth-century plantations generally are seen (by white people) as similar to fancy country clubs—appropriate for beautiful wedding ceremonies and children's fun field trips—rather than to work-death camps (Sullivan 2019). But try instead thinking of a plantation as like Auschwitz, and then imagine happy white adults and children enjoying its historic buildings and lush green lawns. (Yes, Auschwitz has those too.) The sadism of this scene is breathtaking: the sheer pleasure being taken in someone else's intense pain and death. White people don't like to be thought of as sadists, of course. They like to be thought of as morally good people and upstanding citizens, which is part of how white privilege operates fairly invisibly nowadays. White privilege allows, even encourages, white people to inhumanely enjoy pleasures that are dependent on the suffering of Black and other non-white people.

To realize you have skin in the game as a white

person, both structurally and personally, is to realize that you are analogous to a guard in the infamous Stanford Prison Experiment. Conducted in California in 1971, the experiment was run by a Stanford University psychologist who wanted to study the psychological effects of imprisonment (Zimbardo 1999–2019). It was composed of eighteen college student volunteers, who were equally divided into "prisoners" and "guards." While it was supposed to last two weeks, the experiment had to be ended after six days because of the dangerous emotional effects on the nine prisoners, who became depressed and exhibited signs of extreme stress. Just as significant, however, were the emotional and psychological effects on the guards. They gradually took up their assigned roles with gusto and became increasingly cruel. They began to relish their power over the prisoners and to inflict not just physical but also psychological punishment on them. The student-guards were not chosen because they had previous psychological issues or because they seemed or were thought to be sadistic. Nor did they particularly want to play the role of guard. In fact, most of the student volunteers initially wanted to be prisoners. But after several days in an organized system that gave them a great deal of relatively unlimited power over people who were structurally vulnerable to them, the student-guards became twisted into awful people.

Likewise, white privilege and other forms of racial injustice tend to make white people awful. No analogy is perfect, of course, and the results of this particular experiment have not been replicated. But the experiment still works as a heuristic for thinking about white people—and I mean *all* white people, including the "regular" or "good" ones, not just avowed white supremacists. White privilege and white supremacy might seem like opposites, but they are opposed in the way that two sides of the same coin are opposed. They accomplish the same things; white privilege just does it in a politer manner than the overt viciousness of white supremacy. In this way, both white privilege and white supremacy warp white people. Like white supremacy, white privilege is an organized system that psychologically and emotionally harms white people, as well as people of color. I do not mean this as a comparison with the harm that racial injustice does to people of color, and I am not claiming that white people are racially oppressed. There are different kinds and degrees of harm caused by racial injustice. But it's important to note that white people's selves—or as W. E. B. Du Bois (1999) would say, their "white souls"—are being negatively affected by white privilege even when white privilege financially benefits white people. What is particularly insidious about white privilege is that it hides the awfulness of white people, often with a sophisticated veneer of moral goodness. In turn, white people's awfulness, their corroded souls, makes them dangerous to others.

But let's be even more honest still. These last three paragraphs assume that white people *want* to recognize that they have skin in the game, and many of them do not. They probably won't say it that bluntly (that would look bad), but they don't want to experience or perhaps even to know about the pain and harm of racial injustice. It's somewhat understandable; no one wants to be in pain. Why would you want to acknowledge that you're in a game in which you suffer? Maybe no one ever really chooses that. Maybe you either find yourself slapped in the face with that realization, or you don't. For now, I would say that if you won't or can't recognize that your skin is in the game, then you at least can be honest about this—with yourself, even if with no one else. And in that case, you should get out of the way. Get out of the way of people of color, who know how to care for themselves and their communities and don't need white people tripping them up or telling them how to live.

"Help people of color"

Again, this is not about white guilt. It's about a type of action. Getting out of the way isn't enough in the total scheme of things, of course. White people made the mess, and they need to help clean it up. But if they can't do that, if all they can do is keep adding more crap to the mess, then at least it would help for them—for us, for me—to realize this and get out of the way.

This all probably sounds pretty selfish. It might sound like I'm claiming that white people should think only about themselves and not about people of color. Actually, I *am* claiming something like that, but in a different way than the typical accusation of selfishness works. I am not saying that white people should self-interestedly cultivate and enjoy their racial privileges. But I do think that white people need to think a whole lot more about themselves as *white* people and to focus less on people of color and how they can help them. "Helping" those who are "less fortunate" often is not a virtue to cultivate. It can be a temptation to resist. It can trap white people in toxic goodness, and it does so by wielding a false dichotomy between selfishness and selflessness. "Selfishly" focusing on oneself and "selflessly" focusing on other people are not diametrically opposed, as we often think they are. Sometimes the best way that you can "selflessly" help change someone else's life is to "selfishly" try to change your own.

But haven't white people been focusing on themselves far too much already? Isn't *that* precisely the problem? Again, the answer depends on what kind of focus we're talking about. There certainly are ways for white people to be interested in and focused on themselves that maintain white silence, white colorblindness, and white privilege. Their self-interest can be about "just us" in ways that harm or take advantage of other people. But avoiding that problem doesn't necessarily mean always focusing on people of color—it shouldn't mean this. There's a kind of avoidance at work in many white people's lives in which they don't want to think about their own whiteness (when they are willing to think about race at all). That avoidance is as much a part of the problem of white privilege as anything else is. Ture and Hamilton (1992, 81) said it best as part of their observation that Black people needed to think about new values and goals for themselves: "the same holds true for white people of good will; they too need to redefine themselves and their role." White people cannot recognize their skin in the game of racial justice if they aren't willing to (re)examine themselves as white.

To think about new values for themselves, white

people need to break the white silence and figure out how to be white without requiring the existence of a "lower" group against which to implicitly or explicitly compare themselves. This is simultaneously the simplest and the hardest thing to ask of white people, and it's also the main takeaway with which I want to end this book. So, let me say it again. It is simple: white people need to learn how to be merely one race among others (Alcoff 2015). This doesn't mean eliminating whiteness; it doesn't mean that white people would be worse or lower than any other group. They just would *be*, period, along with other racial groups. But this is *the* most challenging thing to ask of a racial group that historically has always been positioned as higher than other racial groups and that has based its self-worth on that comparatively higher position.

I'm willing to bet that this description of white people holds up globally. The United States was built on the conviction that its "real" (white and middle-to-upper-class) citizens needed someone to look down on (Isenberg 2016; see also Hochschild 2016), but the United States is not unique in this respect. The superiority of white people is an implicit or unconscious conviction that holds sway in many historically and currently white dominated countries. The recent example of Sweden is a case

113

in point. It turns out that the so-called Nordic Miracle—the liberal/socialist utopia of prosperity, happiness, goodness, and multicultural openness— was a mirage. It depended on most if not all Swedish citizens being white. With large numbers of people from the Middle East, Africa, and Eastern Europe immigrating to Sweden, the far-right anti-immigrant Sweden Democrats party gained 18 percent of the vote in 2018 elections and will have significant influence in Sweden's parliament as its third largest party (Henley 2018). A nation that once thought that issues of race and racism didn't particularly apply to them—"that's a problem they have in America, not here"—is now having to shed its colorblindness and reckon with its whiteness.

So far, this hasn't been very pretty—not in America, not in Sweden, not in any other predominantly white country that I can think of. There is increasing empirical evidence for what has long been known anecdotally about dominant groups: they feel victimized when they are required or "forced" (perhaps by "liberal government") to share power or resources with oppressed groups (Stanley 2018, 94–95). Frankly, to this point, white people's engagement in the game mostly reveals that they are passionately committed to white privilege and white supremacy. Will that ever change? Will white people ever want to redefine themselves so that they have something different at stake when it comes to racial justice? I do not have answers to these questions. But I do know that something different would happen if white people could at least honestly ask them. If they—if we—cannot do that, then white people likely will remain mired in toxic whiteness, whether in the form of white supremacy or white privilege. That would be bad news for everyone. To paraphrase James Baldwin (1966), until white people no longer need "lesser" people of color to feel good about themselves, then not just America but the entire world is in danger.

References

Alcoff, L. M. (2015). *The Future of Whiteness*. Cambridge, UK: Polity Press.

Alcoff, L. M. (2016). "Skin in the Game: Whiteness without White Supremacy." *The Los Angeles Book Review* [online]. Available at https://lareviewofbooks.org/article/skin-game-whiteness-without-white-supremacy/#!

Ashkenas, J., H. Park, and A. Pearce. (2017). "Even With Affirmative Action, Blacks and Hispanics Are More Underrepresented at Top Colleges Than 35 Years Ago." *The New York Times* [online]. Available at https://www.nytimes.com/interactive/2017/08/24/us/affirmative-action.html

Baldwin, J. (1966). "Unnameable Objects, Unspeakable Crimes." In *The White Problem in America*. Ed. *Ebony* editors. Chicago, IL: Johnson Publishing.

Braden, A. (1999). *The Wall Between*. Knoxville: The University of Tennessee Press.

References

Byrne, D. (2017). "White Guilt Invades Elite Illinois High School." *The Weekly Standard* [online]. Available at https://www.weeklystandard.com/dennis-byrne/white-guilt-invades-elite-illinois-high-school

Clark, A. (2018). *The Poisoned City: Flint's Water and the American Urban Tragedy.* New York: Metropolitan Books.

Coates, T. (2010). "The Arrest of Henry Louis Gates." *The Atlantic* [online]. Available at https://www.theatlantic.com/national/archive/2010/08/the-arrest-of-henry-louis-gates/61365/

Crenshaw, K. (1991). "Mapping the Margins: Intersectionality, Identity Politics, and Violence Against Women of Color." *Stanford Law Review* 43(6): 1241–1299.

Crosley-Corcoran, G. (2014). "Explaining White Privilege to a Broke White Person." *Huffington Post* [online]. Available at http://www.huffingtonpost.com/gina-crosleycorcoran/explaining-white-privilege-to-a-broke-white-person_b_5269255.html

DiAngelo, R. (2018). *White Fragility: Why It's So Hard for White People to Talk About Racism.* Boston, MA: Beacon Press.

Donnelly, K. (2018). *How Political Correctness Is Destroying Australia.* Melbourne: Wilkinson Publishing.

Du Bois, W. E. B. (1994). *The Souls of Black Folk.* Mineola, NY: Dover Publications.

References

Du Bois, W. E. B. (1999). *Darkwater: Voices from Within the Veil*. New York: Harcourt Brace.

Fleming, C. M. (2018). *How To Be Less Stupid About Race*. Boston, MA: Beacon Press.

Foster, D. (2017). "A Guide to White Privilege for White People Who Think They Never Had Any." *Huffington Post* [online]. Available at https://www.huffingtonpost.com/deborah-foster/a-guide-to-white-privileg_b_8526506.html

Gates, Jr., H. L. (2013). "Exactly How 'Black' is Black America?" *The Root* [online]. Available at https://www.theroot.com/exactly-how-Black-is-Black-america-1790895185

Gathright, J. (2018). "Forget Wealth and Neighborhood. The Racial Income Gap Persists." *NPR* [online]. Available at https://www.npr.org/sections/codeswitch/2018/03/19/594993620/forget-wealth-and-neighborhood-the-racial-income-gap-persists

Gibson, J. J. (1979). *The Ecological Approach to Visual Perception*. Boston: Houghton Mifflin Harcourt.

Godoy, M. (2018). "Food Stall Serves Up A Social Experiment: White Customers Asked To Pay More." *National Public Radio* [online]. Available at https://www.npr.org/sections/thesalt/2018/03/02/590053856/food-stall-serves-up-a-social-experiment-charge-white-customers-more-than-minori

Goodman, J. D. (2015). "Officer in James Blake Arrest Used Excessive Force, Panel Says." *New York*

References

Times [online]. Available at https://www.nytimes.com/2015/10/08/nyregion/officer-in-james-blake-arrest-used-excessive-force-panel-says.html

Hayes-Greene, D., and B. Love. (2016). "Measuring Racial Equity: A Groundwater Approach." Cleveland, April 19–20.

Henley, J. (2018). "Sweden Election: Far Right Makes Gains as Main Blocs Deadlocked." *The Guardian* [online]. Available at https://www.theguardian.com/world/2018/sep/09/swedish-election-far-right-on-course-for-sizeable-gains-in-vote

Hochschild, A. R. (2018). *Strangers in Their Own Land: Anger and Mourning on the American Right*. New York: The New Press.

Holmes, A. (2018). "Black With (Some) White Privilege." *New York Times* [online] p. SR1. Available at https://www.nytimes.com/2018/02/10/opinion/sunday/Black-with-some-white-privilege.html

Icanseethruyou. (2012a). "Black Privilege Checklist" [online]. Available at https://icanseethruyou.wordpress.com/2012/06/24/152/

Icanseethruyou. (2012b). "White Privilege?!? Really?!?" [online]. Available at https://icanseethruyou.wordpress.com/2012/03/12/white-privilege-really/

Isenberg, N. (2016). *White Trash: The 400-Year Untold History of Class in America*. New York: Viking.

Lacy, K. (2007). *Blue-Chip Black: Race, Class and Status*

References

in the New Middle Class. Berkeley: The University of California Press.

Lester, M. (2008). Cartoon printed in the *Centre Daily Times*, State College, PA, April 15, 2008.

Lewis, A. E. (2003). "Some Are More Equal than Others: Lessons on Whiteness from School." In *White Out: The Continuing Significance of Racism*. Eds. A. W. Doane and E. Bonilla-Silva. New York: Routledge.

Lind, M. (1998). "The Beige and the Black." *New York Times* [online]. Available at https://www.nytimes.com/1998/08/16/magazine/the-beige-and-the-black.html

Lorde, A. (1984). *Sister Outsider: Essays and Speeches*. New York: The Crossing Press.

McIntosh, P. (1989). "White Privilege: Unpacking the Invisible Knapsack." *Peace and Freedom* July/August: 10–12.

Masuoka, N., and J. Junn. (2013). *The Politics of Belonging: Race, Public Opinion, and Immigration*. Chicago: The University of Chicago Press.

May, V. (2015). *Pursuing Intersectionality, Unsettling Dominant Imageries*. New York: Routledge.

Mills, C. (2007). "The Racial Contract and Beyond." Presentation made at Penn State University, July 25.

New Trier High School. (2017). All-School Seminar Day 2017 [online]. Available at http://www.newtrier.k12.il.us/seminarday/ and http://www.newtrier.k12.

References

il.us/Student_Services/Adviser_Program/All-School_Se minar_Day/All-School_Seminar_Day_FAQ/

Preston, J. (2009). *Whiteness and Class in Education*. Dordrecht, The Netherlands: Springer.

Raffo, S. (2009). "White Noise: White Adults Raising White Children to Resist White Supremacy" [online]. Available at http://myfeetonlywalkforward.blogspot. com/2009/08/white-noise-white-adults-raising-white. html

Rifkin, M. (2017). *Beyond Settler Time: Temporal Sovereignty and Indigenous Self-Determination*. Durham, NC: Duke University Press.

Roberts, D. (2002). *Shattered Bonds: The Color of Child Welfare*. New York: Basic Books.

Robinson, C. L. (2011). "Hair as Race: Why 'Good Hair' May Be Bad for Black Females." *Howard Journal of Communications* 22(4): 358–376.

Scheff, T. J. (2000). "Shame and the Social Bond: A Sociological Theory." *Sociological Theory* 18(1): 84–99.

Shapiro, B. (2015). "Why White People Seek Black Privilege." *Breitbart* [online]. Available at http://www. breitbart.com/big-government/2015/08/19/why-whi te-people-seek-black-privilege-2/

Sommers, S. and M. Norton. (2016). "White People Think Racism Is Getting Worse. Against White People." *The Washington Post* [online]. Available at https://www. washingtonpost.com/posteverything/wp/2016/07/21/

References

white-people-think-racism-is-getting-worse-against-w
hite-people/?noredirect=on&utm_term=.2c926bd1f
23f

Sonnie, A., and J. Tracy. (2011). *Hillbilly Nationalists, Urban Race Rebels, and Black Power: Community Organizing in Radical Times*. Brooklyn, NY: Melville House Publishing.

Spirit. (n.d.). Hillbilly Teeth [online]. Available at https://www.spirithalloween.com/product/hillbilly-tee th/46804.uts

Srivastava, S. (2006). "Tears, Fears and Careers: Anti-Racism and Emotion in Social Movement Organizations." *The Canadian Journal of Sociology* 31(1): 55–90.

Stanley, J. (2018). *How Fascism Works: The Politics of Us and Them*. New York: Random House.

Sullivan, S. (2006). *Revealing Whiteness: The Unconscious Habits of Racial Privilege*. Bloomington: Indiana University Press.

Sullivan, S. (2014). *Good White People: The Problem with Middle-Class White Anti-Racism*. Albany, NY: SUNY Press.

Sullivan, S. (2017). "White Priority." *Critical Philosophy of Race* 5(2): 171–182.

Sullivan, S. (2019). "Becoming White: White Children and the Erasure of Black Suffering." In *Race as Phenomena: Between Phenomenology and Philosophy of Race*. Ed. Emily Lee. Lanham, MD: Rowman and Littlefield.

References

Tangney, J. P. (1995). "Recent Advances in the Empirical Study of Shame and Guilt." *American Behavioral Science* 38(3): 1132–1145.

Tha God, C. (2017). *Black Privilege: Opportunity Comes to Those Who Create It*. New York: Touchstone.

Ture, K., and C. V. Hamilton. (1992). *Black Power: The Politics of Liberation in America*. Second Edition. New York: Vintage Books.

Underhill, M. R. (2017). "Parenting during Ferguson: Making Sense of White Parents' Silence." *Ethnic and Racial Studies* 41(11): 1934–1951.

Velotti, P., C. Garofalo, F. Bottazzi, and V. Caretti. (2016). "Faces of Shame: Implications for Self-Esteem, Emotion Regulation, Aggression, and Well-Being." *The Journal of Psychology: Interdisciplinary and Applied* 151(2): 171–184.

Zack, N. (2015). *White Privilege and Black Rights: The Injustice of U.S. Police Racial Profiling and Homicide*. Lanham, MD: Rowman and Littlefield.

Zimbardo, P. G. (1999–2019). Stanford Prison Experiment [online]. Available at http://www.prison exp.org/